PARTY OF 2

PATH TO UNION

VITO MUCCI

Acknowledgments

In my first book, I acknowledged that everything I do is a footnote to my love for Claudia … and that fact does not escape my mind for a single second in any day. In this book, I have to say that Claudia was literally the source of all my knowledge, as my experiences with her have reshaped my entire understanding of the dynamics of men and women and given me the ability to test out every tool and theory in real-life situations. I acknowledge her gorgeous elemental soul, her passionate heart, her impulsive creativity, and her willingness to be present for all the violent and messy processes that this incarnation provides.

I want to thank my amazing mother, as well, for giving me a sense of wonder regarding the Divine Feminine and telling me fables and stories that honored those depths. She also surrounded me with enough of the Divine Masculine from multiple angles for me to have models to aspire to and highlighted their qualities for me. Without those mythic connections being modeled in reality, I would not be who I am.

I also want to thank my first book, *Coffee for Consciousness 101: The Application of Perspective to Reality* for DEMANDING that I bring it into being. I am also thankful I learned a lot about typos during that book … saved me a lot of time in this one.

I want to thank everyone who opens their heart, who trusts, who tries, even though the odds are low and the risk is high. You all truly are the pioneers of the heart and the impassioned forces behind the evolution of the human consciousness.

I also need to shout out to my love song heroes … Jeff Buckley, Deftones, The Cure, Tricky, Zero 7, and Radiohead in the world of music. Want to thank everyone involved in *The Piano*, *Fight Club*, and *Groundhog Day* in the world of film.

I want to thank all of my exes … and all of Claudia's exes (especially my husband-in-law, Mr. Wheeler, whom I have the honor of co-parenting with).

Finally, I want to thank the collectively emerging Divine Masculine and Feminine for giving this book an audience.

Table of Contents

Foreword

Bless your heart. Bless your heart by opening it and letting the flood of emotion crush you and spill out into the world.

Bless your body. Bless your engaged presence with the possibility of rapture through experience and deep connection ... let that risk be your first reward as you step into the Sun.

Bless your mind. Bless its skill and intellect and all the mechanisms of control that have kept us safe on our journey to get to where we are, the point where our survival must give way to our ability to consciously thrive in a co-created world.

Bless your journey. Bless the desires and holy impulses as they pull you through the garden and the brambles and the ruins of civilizations toward rapturous expansion.

Bless your world. Bless the people you work and live with and the people you share space with ... even the people you shop with.

Bless everything. Bless everything affecting everything dancing and entwining and spiraling out into the void against all odds.

Bless your love. Bless the actions you take to hone your skills to honor the beautiful feelings within you.

Thank you ... bless you.

Chapter 1:

Evolution ... Unleashing the Human Heart

Welcome to the garden!

It may not be as inviting as my normal greeting, *"Welcome to the playground,"* but for the purposes of this endeavor it is much more accurate. I like accurate.

Gardens are labors of love. They do not just sustain life through the fruits they bear, but they create a harmonious relationship between us and the Earth. This may not seem as vitally important as it is, because *we are used to seeing gardens*. But what I am going to propose in this book, while sharing many traits with gardening, is not something we see often ... or ever.

What I am going to propose during the course of this book is how we can evolve into a heightened ability to connect, specifically in relationships. But before I jump into the mess of men and women, we need to first look at the tool we will be using to implement these ideas: the human mind.

I wrote a book on the human mind, so please understand that I am just giving a snapshot here, but what I am saying we need to look at is *the relationship between the human heart and the human mind*. How much of our mind is regarding the desires and needs of the heart? How much of it is serving the needs of egoic fear? The mind will be dominated by some internal motivational force. To create a mind more capable of connecting with others, a healthy relationship with the heart is necessary. That allows the heart to dominate, rather than allowing egoic fear to do so.

Here's a visual aid … picture the heart and mind on opposite sides of a dance floor, both trying to work up the guts to meet up in the middle. The mind is masculine (intent and energy), the heart feminine (allowance and growth). **The ego is the guy's super-needy wingman**, convincing him it's not worth the risk over and over … *forever*. Why? Because the ego hates change and not being in control of the mind. It is seductive and almost always gets its way, until the mind gets on the dance floor and *forms a stronger relationship with his dance partner than he ever had with his fear.* That's an evolution of consciousness.

All throughout this book, the movement away from ego domi-nance and into heart dominance is going to be at the forefront. That is the only way we can learn to trust our heart, *and in turn to trust others with it.* That is what is needed to move forward.

Why is this level of trust necessary to move forward?

Because our job here … our purpose at this time in human history … is to "unleash the human heart" and learn how to use the tools of our mind to protect the heart from the clutches of our fear-based egoic mind.

When the Power of Love Overcomes the Love of Power

"When the Power of Love Overcomes the Love of Power the world will know peace." – Jimi Hendrix

I always loved this quote. I thought it was catchy and could be meaningful for every level of intellect, as well as serving the purpose of putting forth love as the primary goal. But … I didn't realize the full significance until a few years ago, because I hadn't yet started to look into primary motivations and the determining factors for the behavior of the world at large. There is a huge history in support of following the "love of power." It exists because we're scared to death. We're not scared of marauding tigers anymore (especially not now, as they rarely run amok in our neighborhoods); we're scared of opening our hearts to a chaotic and uncertain world.

The issue is not that we love power as a species because it looks cool or feels good. It doesn't really feel like much of anything except SAFETY (and later numbness). But safety from what? Safety from the uncertainty of fully experiencing life and risking being hurt.

D'oh!

The Power of Love lies in risking our hearts ... because the *joy of doing so* is more powerful than our *fear of being hurt*. That is the Power of Love. It is not a singular thing, not a feeling. It is a commitment and an attitude about HOW TO LIVE in a world that is frightening. The Power of Love is not a "thing" that exists external to us. **It IS US**. It is us, when we are at our best and most courageous.

When we are at our best and most courageous, we don't need power. Then, the "Love of Power" goes away naturally. The only reason it persists in such a stubborn fashion is that we have not set social precedent in this area ... YET. We haven't shown ourselves that the "Power of Love" overcomes the "Love of Power" NATURALLY and *has much better results*. That, mixed with the fact that it is really frightening to risk our hearts, is the reason we need to put a lot more effort into bringing this issue forward.

When I was young and thought of "peace" within the confines of the quote, I thought it meant world peace. As in, when mean power mongers and war profiteers were confronted by us hippies and New Agers they would at some point lose their ability to create a system of global cruelty and violence … and maybe that's true. But that's not what I see now.

What do I see now?

The peace that is the toughest to come by is the internal peace that exists when WE make our OWN peace with the internal war for power and control that our mind wages over the desires of our hearts.

As within, so without? I think it would work that way. I mean, I definitely don't see it working from the outside-in. Do you? Can you imagine a power monger-type person just being persuaded to give up their entire value system by something outside of themselves? I can't. Why would they? That's self-annihilating behavior. But if we start becoming the Peace that exists when the Power of Love overcomes the Love of Power, it's going to be difficult to deny the example we set.

Now, I'm not saying that opening our hearts on the individual level will change the world … wait … yes, I am. And I'm not just saying that it will, **I'm saying it's the only thing that will**. All other distractions and abstractions, no matter how attractive, are not going to get it done.

Now it's time to get into why that's the case.

The difficulties at the core of this issue (unleashing the human heart) are tens of thousands of years in the making. The fear that corrals us and keeps us safe from risk is the same fear that kept us cautious and alive in the caveman days … that kept us suspicious of anything that was new and different ... kept us ALIVE. That sets a tough precedent to overthrow.

On every level of social consciousness, we are in a position of needing to overthrow ideologies that have been in place since we came out of caves and started forming societies. That's where we are. The ego-based fear matrix in our minds wants us to survive, while the heart wants us to thrive. Unfortunately, the ego-based systems are ignorant of something important. They have NO IDEA that we're not in any actual danger anymore. And moreover? The ego- based systems are defending the HEART from injury, when in fact, the human heart is IMMORTAL.

History Lessons ... and the Egoic Override

From the beginning of history, pain has been a signal that injury was occurring. It was a signal to hide, recover, protect, and heal. The human mind has naturally built-in systems to ensure that this response occurs. That is what **Body Sovereignty** is about, a term I spoke of in CFC101. Survival comes first. Period. And throughout the many thousands of years getting to this point in time, those who did not have this implanted security system were likely weeded out of the gene pool.

The issue we face now is that this truly "reflex" response, which has served its purpose, needs to be adjusted.

The adjustment that needs to take place is the *separation of emotional pain from physical pain*. If physical pain is occurring, we definitely still need to mind our body and get some healing done. If emotional pain is occurring? We're not actually in *danger* anymore. We may need to observe and process emotion, but fight or flight isn't really appropriate in these situations in the 21st century.

Were we ever in danger from emotional pain? Yes. We were. And this is why it was hardwired in along with physical pain to ensure our survival.

Also? The reflex itself is different. Where physical pain forces us to hide and recover, emotional pain causes us to shut down our feelings. That is the OPPOSITE of healing and recovering. I'm going to list some times and places and how emotional shutdown was necessary in an attempt to show why it is NOT necessary now.

Caves: The amount of loss during this time period did not allow for close bonding. If one was too attached and lost a child or mate, if they couldn't just move on like a sociopath, their genes would not continue. Pretty simple.

Egypt/Greece/Rome: During this time period, we had a slave class and a ruling elite class. The slave class was deeply suffering, so they didn't get an opportunity to open their hearts. Why did the elite class not have the opportunity? Because opening their hearts meant empathizing with the slaves, and that was too painful. Some would argue that they didn't think of it that way, that they were supposed to be "better than" … but their hearts knew. All hearts know pain.

Middle Ages: During this time of horror, everything was about power and dominance. Righteous warring and brutality. I cannot believe we survived it, honestly.

Renaissance: Art and culture came forward … more safety was achieved. But cultures were still religion-dominant and the socialized world was fighting to form boundaries and countries. No time for love Dr. Jones (and we certainly didn't have time to prioritize feelings).

Colonial to Industrial to the '60s: Now the excuses are wearing thin. There's a LOT of safety. We're still in a state of struggling to dominate on the social level, and money has become a sort of twisted new religion, but we're pretty capable of forming bonds with people and risking our vulnerable selves to connect. By the end of this period we're starting to see that we can expand our minds and engage new feelings and attitudes, culminating in the protests and changes of the '60s. The '60s were the first time in human history that Love and Peace were popular slogans. That was only fifty years ago. Most of the equality and personal freedom that they were fighting for hasn't even come to fruition yet.

Now: We're safe, with tons of freedom, and no real threat of scarcity (even though we do still have some social problems). And while Peace and Love are still sweet slogans, we haven't really expanded their use to engage our psychological frailty. That same frailty that leads to a 70% divorce rate and a deeply unsatisfied collection of highly socialized people. We just can't get it together.

Why?

The same reason that the pharaohs couldn't. The pain is fierce, and there is no obvious need to push ourselves through it. It does not seem to us that our survival depends on it, so we are not forced to open up to a chaotic world *against our nature* with *no guarantee of success*. The Egoic Override wins. And it wins easily.

So why must it not win? What's the big freaking deal anyway? OUR SURVIVAL ACTUALLY DEPENDS ON IT. Oops.

The fact that it's not obvious that our survival depends on it is a real issue, but it doesn't change the truth. Our survival depends on us opening our hearts. All the stages of growth and evolution of social culture have gotten us to a point where the only two frontiers left to address are the internal world of the Heart-Mind Connection … and outer space. While NASA may be having us think the next in line is outer space … it has to be the Heart-Mind connection.

We have evolved into safety, and out of scarcity. We have evolved out of tribal warring and formed cultures. We have also evolved to the point where we can and will overwhelm the Earth with waste, overpopulate, and breed ourselves out of existence. That is IF WE DO NOT BEGIN TO FORM A HARMONIC CONNECTION WITH EACH OTHER AND THE PLANET WE LIVE ON.

We have to open our hearts to fully empathize with our fellow man and the planet. If we don't do that, we're going to be likely candidates for the endangered species list. Besides the empathy we need to not blow each other up, we need to find methods of creating energy and making waste that don't make the planet uninhabitable. We're going to HAVE *to let go of our need to control* to survive. We have to share and compromise, and that means opening the heart. This is how we become stewards of the planet and take on an active role in our own evolution.

Chapter 2:

Binary Synergy:
A Love Story of Ones and Zeroes

I love creation. Love it.

From my earliest years I have enjoyed using my mind to form combinations of stories and humor and knowledge. I remember that each time I would come across new concepts, I would allow infinite changes and translations to grow from a single understanding. I. Love. Creating. Love it.

The most mind-blowing of these conceptual expansions, in my youth, was binary code. Binary code, as I first understood it, was just as a number system in base two. Just ones and zeroes. "Why would anyone do that?" was my immediate question ... then I learned what it was used for.

Ones and Zeroes ... 1 + 1 = Infinity

Binary code is the language used by computers. It is the foundation of all programming. It manages everything from alarm clocks to Space missions. Binary code, in this instance, is proof of something. That proof is what blew my mind as a child.

Using just a "1" and a "0" ... a limitless amount of sophisticated and expansive realities are possible. Two things, when used complementarily, become *more* than the sum of their parts. This is **Synergy**. 1 + 1 = 3 ... at LEAST 3. The two components are added together and a set of outcomes far beyond the static math are created.

1 and 0 do not make two characters ... they make a language and everything that language accomplishes as a result of their existence.

Man and woman *do not make a couple*. They make a family, and every bit of growth and experience flows from that. Family, like binary code, is closer to a language than a simple "coupling."

The combination of living beings, the consciousness and experiences that bring the world to life, is more than a math problem. It is an exercise in the creation of Synergy.

Do we achieve it, though? If so, to what extent? Are we HAPPY with the myriad of creations our connections have brought into our lives? Those are the questions that need answering, because the quality of our lives is directly dependent on those answers.

What is the *quality* ... of our engagement in *duality*?

Duality is an idea that has been judged from many sides. Good, bad, ugly, illusory, etc. It's generally seen now as a bad thing ... a separation. The separation from God/Source and our individual separation from each other is the cause of much distress, much conflict, much suffering. But this separation *is also an Opportunity*. That Opportunity is what I believe life to be about. The polarization of duality is not so that we mourn the distance between the things of this world, *but that we overcome that distance*.

Duality and Bridge-building

What do you think of when you hear the word "duality"? My natural inclination is a negative feeling, a separating distance … like I am on one side of a river and someone else is on the other. It's a bummer.

Maybe your initial reaction is similar, maybe not. But my *initial reaction* is not what my **final response** to that situation is. That situation, being on opposite sides of a river, is not about how far apart we are, but **how to find a way** to get together regardless of that.

I know from personal experience how much distance can be traversed when we really want to close gaps of separation between ourselves and others (people, ideas, etc.). I know how desire can be creative and how duality and distance can be *an inspirational challenge* to engage *courageously*. I know how being separated from the woman I loved could make me create entire new areas within myself and in the world … and I know that the tiny bits of separation that exist between us now are continually driving me to learn and discover the worlds of information and glory that exist within her.

Always-be-building-bridges. That's what duality can inspire us to do. It can inspire us to find ways of overcoming duality and creating connection. Maybe that is the purpose of duality in some universally organized sense, but I am not

INTERESTED in purpose. I am just interested in the joy I get from engaging in the *opportunity*. The opportunity is swimming, building bridges, learning how to COMMUNICATE even though there is distance between us … these all are available, and they give deep satisfaction when we commit to the process of CONNECTING to someone.

It's all about that on this Earth plane. Connection. There is nothing as glorious and resonant as a connected moment. It is as close to immortality as we get, carving out a moment or experience so deeply alongside another consciousness in such a way that it pulses like a beating heart. Deep down, we know this. This is why we yearn for it. This is why we must take our opportunities as they present themselves and use whatever tools available to close the gaps in our separation.

I look into the eyes of my mate and I feel **home**. Even then, in that deep comfort, there is still opportunity to get closer … as "even between the closest souls, infinite distances still remain." This is why the inspiration never ends, why deep desire between two people is a creative force that is unmatched in the rest of reality. It leads to connection and conjures all the tools that are actively necessary in maintaining it. The tools we find, the languages we learn, and the structures we build to overcome the distance between ourselves and our desires … all of that is not just something available to us, but something that is available to everyone should they wish to use the example we set.

This ends up being a quest … not unlike the quest for the Holy Grail, which symbolized the connection to God, the quest we are on in this lifetime is the quest to connect to the "**Divine Other**" … the object of our heart's desire, regardless of whether it is friendship or love or ideas or creation or

God--it doesn't matter. The quest to find and know the Divine Other is the point of existence, as it is the natural drive of all individuated beings to seek it.

The purpose of duality is to overcome duality. It's all about the bridges we create and the fleeting moments that take our breath away after we do so.

"The meeting of two personalities is like the contact of two chemical substances. If there is any reaction, both are transformed." - Jung

We want reactions.

The juicy goodness exists in the differences that duality provides. Duality is not the enemy. It is not just in overcoming duality that we find deep meaning. *It also exists in enjoying the aspects of duality that cannot exist in a unified state.* There is no "touch" if there is no "difference."

The deliciousness ... everything existing outside of us is an opportunity for sensation and richness through connection. Richness is spoken of often, but not often directly tied to the quality of life we have, which is where it belongs. Depth of *experience*, of *impact*, of *resonance* ... that is what richness brings us.

Why does all of this relate directly to quality of life? Because, while connecting to the Divine Other creates limitless familial realities and a language to go along with it, the lack thereof ... is hell. Numb, pointless, hell.

The Hell of Separation … a God-Forsaken land.

My mother was a badass. She taught me tons growing up, and I owe the foundation of my knowledge to her. I once asked her what hell was, having overheard kids on the playground at school, and having only a shallow idea of what on Earth they thought it could mean that made it so scary to them. My mother was quite good at skipping gore, especially when it was unnecessary to make the point, so she went about describing hell to me by giving the heart of the matter.

She told me that hell was Separation from God (she said "The Divine" at the time). Now THAT scared me. Demons and guts would have made me say "EW!" but the idea of being separated from God? That … was scary. Then she told me something scarier. She told me that most people on this planet were so afraid and defensive that they isolated themselves from God, their home, and their family. We can do it to ourselves while we're alive. That's scary.

This is, of course, basically what I see now. It's one of the main reasons why I am writing this book. This is a God-Forsaken Land. I don't see connections. I see a world more defined by separation than connection. I see people living out of harmony with the world around them and the world inside themselves. This isn't just an inability to form intimate connections with others that creates hell, it is an internal private hell I see running through almost everyone. We are, as a species coming towards evolution, in the "hell of Separation." That is our base state of being right now. While there are parts of the world that behave more cruelly as a result of this than others, the fact of the matter doesn't change. Most of us are living in hell.

Sounds like it may be too strong a description. But … isn't that what it feels like to you? Isn't that what it feels like when there is a deep miscommunication between yourself and a loved one? Doesn't it feel like that when we feel betrayed by our parents or family? Doesn't it feel like that when the world is unfair or unjust or uncaring? Doesn't it feel like that when we get home *and we don't feel like we're home, or that we will ever get home*?

There are certainly worse feelings than separation and loneliness. Torture, from what I understand, is really painful (and to think, I have issues just getting teeth pulled). But the hell of separation does something even torture can't. It makes life meaningless. It makes goals unimportant. It makes self-improvement "wasted time." It dampens joy and *deadens senses*. And … life doesn't have to be that way. Not at all.

We don't have to live in hell. We just have to commit ourselves to connecting … *no matter what it takes.*

I know I'm going to be making points for moving forward in relationships and trying to connect more deeply and intimately … but I'm pretty sure that the contrast I made between "a beautiful language of Family and Creation" and "hell" is unlikely to be topped. But that's how I see this subject, and how I've experienced it first and second hand. So that's how I'm going to share it, and why I'm going to go as directly as I can *into the mess of life* to do so.

I'm going to note again that this doesn't have to include another person; we can be at one with ourselves and the Divine Other WITHIN us (that strange inner elusive beauty). But not being in any relationship? That is what we are trying to keep from happening as we move to unleash the human heart on this beautiful world.

Chapter 3:

The Sun and Earth ... a Love Story

Last chapter we spoke of Binary Code and the synergy created when two divinely different elements are used in concert. In that case, not only was language was created, but the entirety of computerized reality (which is everywhere). What we are looking at in this book is Divine Energy in the masculine and feminine forms. Not surprisingly, most pairings that achieve synergy have masculine and feminine components.

Divine Pairings, like Binary Code, are unit pairings that are "creatively effective" for the Universe as a whole. Yes, the Universe. Any expansive energy on the micro level fuels the expansion of the Universe on the macro. I consider all of these pairings to have a masculine and feminine component (or multitude of components, actually). It may seem like an oversimplification to assign energy types to the forces of nature, but there is nothing simple about the combination of masculine and feminine energy. In this book, I will focus mainly on the man/woman and the mind/heart versions of Divine Pairings because those are the two that most directly affect our lives, in my experience. But there are many versions of Divine Pairings, and highlighting the masculine and feminine in a few of them may give us some fresh perspectives on how mythic our reality actually is.

Because it is mythic. We are mythic. Our internal journey and the journeys we entertain with others ... they are *mythic*.

The Sun and Earth, a Love Story ...

My favorite masculine and feminine Divine Pairing is the one that fuels and houses everything we know. The Sun as masculine ... and the Earth as feminine. Do the Sun and Earth have both masculine and feminine energy? Of course. But in this particular pairing, they play these specific roles *for each other*. And that is how we will be recognizing and speaking of masculine and feminine ... from within a specific closed system, with each component thriving off the presence of the **Divine Other** (that which we are relating to in a specific creative connection).

We look at these from within a closed system because all things in the Universe play different roles for each other, and the umbrellas of definitions we would normally use to define where certain lines should be drawn *are not applicable when the whole of possible reality is in play*. Besides, we want to make people's lives better, so abstracting out is simply unnecessary and confusing when what we are trying to learn is "how to improve the success and depth of connectivity between a Divine Pair."

The Sun: A ball of fiery explosions expressing energy out to the whole of the Universe.

The Earth: A rock, that upon receiving the energy from the Sun, produces luscious sprawling life and gives rise to a collective of Consciousness.

This relationship is bonded by gravity in the same way people are bonded by love. In the movie *Interstellar*, it was postulated that gravity was a form of love being expressed by the Universe itself. Given the nature of Divine Pairings, I am inclined to agree.

Energy is "naturally" released by the Sun, and *any* recipient that can use that energy to create a full world becomes the Divine Other *for the Sun*. And what beautiful gift does our sweet Earth give him and the Universe in return? Life. Consciousness. A vast well of varying species over a unique and rich history … and all he had to do was be unapologetically himself *without holding back*. That is the Presence that is needed for the Divine Masculine component of the Divine Pair. He has to *show up* and *give his all*.

If the Sun stops doing its thing for five minutes? Everyone dies. Billions of living things … gone. Luckily, not as much is asked of us people to keep up our masculine half of the bargain … *as men* we don't have to be perfect, and *as minds protecting an emotive heart* we don't have to be nearly as vigilant.

The Earth's job is to be the Home, the Mother, and the Nurturer … the soil from which the planted seed's fruit grows and blossoms into existence.

In this way, the Sun and Earth play the role of Father and Mother to humankind. This is much closer to the first religions of man, *before social and psychological control became part of the religious focus*.

Sun and Earth, father and mother, masculine and feminine, our fuel and our home.

This is also what we are for each other, whether we know it or not. Our masculine is the energy the feminine uses to create life. It's obvious when we see the sperm-egg-baby process, but less obvious when we see that it is the healthy Divine Masculine energy of the calm and patient mind that allows the feminine of the Heart to bear its desires forth into this brutal reality.

Sun and Earth.

Masculine and Feminine.

Seed and Womb.

Mind and Heart.

Where else can we see these energy pairings? Big Bang and The Universe. Time and Phenomena. Conscious Energy and Life. Energy (vibration) and Matter.

It's a big deal. Pairings, and the resulting realities their combinations create, make up existence. And it is that energy which we are born of and that which we serve by our participation in the richness of connecting to each other on this plane. It is on this plane that our opportunity lies. Not in concept, not in theory, but in engaging the Divine Other that we have the opportunity to connect with RIGHT NOW. Like you and I ... no matter who you are, you and I are in connection right now *as you are reading this*. Everything that changes in life as a result of this connection is what life is about.

We are always in connection. Always in a relationship with every single thing in the Universe, *simply by sharing simultaneous incarnation*. Duality is based on the idea that I am "in here" and everything else is "out there" ... and while some philosophers claim that is an illusory reality, I'd rather stop judging it and see how we can USE it, if it actually is the case.

If I'm "in here" and everything else in existence (including my mind and body) is "out there," what can I do to SOLVE that issue of separation, and in doing so, become better acquainted with my surrounding reality? THAT IS THE QUESTION ... the important one we must ask. I don't care whether there is some illusion in place or not. *The only thing I'm concerned with is how to have a better relationship with everything "out there."*

When I look at that, the rest of the philosophy disintegrates and reduces into a directive, a call to action founded on a desire to connect as deeply as possible with everything.

How Well Do You KNOW It?

What is the nature and quality of our relationship with _____? We need to be able to fill in the blank, and without fear be able to acknowledge how we are consciously relating to anything our focus is engaged with. We use **Observation Consciousness** to do this, the state of observation where Unconditional Positive Regard for the self and others is generated and utilized *for as close to objective truth as we can hope to achieve.*

We may be of the opinion that there are elements of reality we are not in relationship with. This is not true. We are relating to stars giving off light that we will never see. We are relating to every living thing on the planet ... every molecule in existence.

There is a set of questions for dealing with this system in place to make this accurate description understandable. When we look at how we are relating to "_____," we can answer a couple of questions to figure out if there is action we need to take based on how important that relationship is.

For instance …

"How am relating to a star in another galaxy?"

-    I am ignorant of it. My relationship is one of ignorance.

Then we ask, "How important is _____ to my reality (in this case, the star)?"

-    Totally not important at all.

Then we ask, "So, is there anything I need to do to improve that relationship?"

-    Not really.

Now, to show the other end of the spectrum …

"How am I relating to my mate/wife?"

-    I am doing well. My relationship is healthy.

"How important is _____ to my reality?"

-    It's the most important relationship in my life by far.

"So, is there anything I need to do to improve the relationship?

-    Always. Every day.

We need to be able to use Observation Consciousness to acquire which areas need attention, but the *importance of the relationship in question* is what ends up making the demands on our consciousness. "How well do we know it?" doesn't matter so much when we're dealing with things that are distanced from our connections to people and ideas … but when dealing with people we care about, we ALWAYS need to know them better and we ALWAYS need to be engaged in "Inquiry" to find out how we can know them better.

This is a commitment to being observant. Why does it take a commitment? *Because people change every single day.* And if we start *assuming* that we are correctly related to someone *rather than observing*, then our relationship **WILL** go from healthy to IGNORANT really quickly. **WILL**, not *MIGHT*.

Also, there are countless elements to who we are as living people that can be inquired upon. When I think of my mate, I don't think of some generic picture of a being, I think of everything in the world I have observed her caring about, and how well I know THOSE THINGS … not just how well I know her. I do this because EVERYTHING in her reality has an impact on my reality. Everything. That's because she is fully and deeply in my heart.

So when Prince dies, and there's a full-on mourning period, I join her in it, because I have learned how precious that time in her life was. And I learn a LOT about Prince really quickly, because I want to share that with her. I want to see him how she sees him, and feel as close to what she feels as I can.

This is not me being a man and trying to understand a woman, *this is me using the Divine Masculine of my mind to connect more deeply with my own heart*, and her heart, thus allowing the Divine Feminine within myself to experience mourning Prince with her. I don't know Prince like she does. But my heart wants to join her, and my mind offers the fuel. That's how this works.

We will get to have moments forever forward in our relationship when Prince is on the radio, *because I joined her in that*. I was able to do that because I asked the question "What is the quality of my relationship to something my mate cares about?"… found myself to be ignorant of it, and was inspired to take action to improve that.

But what about the other major form of unhealthy relating? We have seen "ignorance," but have not yet taken a close look at "resisting." Resisting is generally the form that takes place during moments of Cognitive Dissonance, a violent reaction in our mind meant to protect us from a reality or feeling that makes us deeply uncomfortable.

This also utilizes Observer Consciousness, but relies on our commitment to *rigorous self-honesty*. As we know, this is a rare quality. Those who understand how important it is are trying to make it sexier ... but it's probably going to take a while. Until then, we should get used to seeing it and using it so that we can model it for others. That way we can show off the positive effects when they happen. The reason that rigorous self-honesty is in play here is that we have to state that something happening inside of us is out of our control and making us uncomfortable. Both of those facts are irritating, to say the least.

The question set for this is different ... Observation Consciousness comes first ... then has to shift from seeing our internal reaction, to seeing our reaction to that reaction, and then measuring our level of discomfort. It's like **Reaction-Ception** with added analysis at the end. Yes, I said Reaction-Ception.

So, the first step is observing the reaction ... this example is of my own internal reaction.

"I am having a random bout of panic" ... that is the Observation. That kicks in a second question.

"Wait, how do I feel about seeing that I'm having this reaction? Am I frustrated? Am I hopeless or depressed? Am I annoyed?"

That stimulates the second round of Observation, the one where we figure out how uncomfortable we are with what we've seen. If our answer is any one of the above (along with a myriad of other descriptive terms), then we are going to be *naturally resistant* to Observing and feeling the emotion. It will be *in our nature* to 1) Hide from seeing it and 2) Escape from the feeling **before we can process it**.

That's information we need to have. We need to know where our blind spots are and where our **Escape Triggers** are. Escape Triggers are moments that make us so internally uncomfortable that we have to withdraw from our Conscious apprehension of it, using one tool or another.

For my Divine Other's emotional realities/reactivities there is another breakdown …

"They are having some sort of meltdown" … that is the Observation. This could be my kids or my mate, and to a lesser extent maybe my mom or brother, but that's it. Therapist/client relationships are not Divine Pairings. This kicks in more questions.

"How comfortable or uncomfortable am I with THEIR emotion?"

People are emotional beings. Those closest to us hopefully feel comfortable enough to let their emotions flow, but that doesn't mean we don't have to do some work to allow them that space. So, how comfortable are we when our kids start screaming? When our mates start crying and cursing and going ballistic? Generally, we are pretty uncomfortable … but that leads to the third question.

"How appropriate is it that I am having issues with something that is going on within another person? And honestly, how helpful is that? Is that the best response we can have?"

It's rarely appropriate, even more rarely helpful, and almost always the first step to resisting their reality and escaping into our own, where we're safe, *exactly when they need us present with them the most.*

The best surfers can still get tossed by big waves, but they never blame the ocean ... that is their Divine Other. They shake the water off and improve their technique, with great humility and reverence. That's how we do this. With our spouses, with our kids, with our families.

In moving consciously through these situations, we are not just being good parents to ourselves and others, we *are sourcing* Divine Masculine and Divine Feminine elements *into our behavioral matrix.* We are becoming the Sun within ourselves, becoming the Earth. We are protecting and being patient, as well as allowing energy, and in doing so using that synergy to create an outcome that serves the highest natures of our soul and the growth of those around us.

But we have to be in Observation Consciousness first, willing to see ourselves clearly, and ask the questions that can lead us to the most helpful behavior. That is where Divine energy gets the opportunity to step forward within us.

I am discussing ignorance and resistance for this amount of time because we do NOT want to have these two aspects present in our Divine Pairings any more than they absolutely have to be. So when we ask ourselves "How well do we know our Divine Other?" we can confidently step forward and say, "As well as I can and getting better every day." Because that's the only answer that can generate happiness within the relationship rather than just getting it by leaching the energy out of a relationship (and it's gonna run out if none is being generated).

The Divine Pairs in nature are not resistant or ignorant … that's why they have been around and in healthy commune so long. It's also why their examples are the best to follow. The Sun is consistent and unselfish, giving warmth and protection. The Earth spins and has her seasons, but uses the Sun's energy to build a world of life. They don't resist each other. The Sun doesn't stop shining and the Earth doesn't stop spinning. That's what we're going after. We're not going to reach that level of consistency, but the idea is that we get as close as possible to it. That's why we use myth to teach lessons, not because we're going to be Knights or Jedi one day, but because we want to get as close to embodying what we love about them as possible.

Embodying Myth

We want our Mind to shine on our Heart, fuel it, and protect it. We want our purpose and energy to shine on those we love, if we are embodying the masculine. We want our being to allow energy to penetrate us and use it to create Home and beauty if we are embodying the feminine. Men and women alike can play either role … and there are many that do. But the energy of masculine and feminine, understanding that the energy itself, the attitude, the natural drive, **that is what creates a gender, rather than gender describing what type of energy we should have**. That is putting the cart before the horse … no pun intended.

The parts and pieces of human beings are symbols. They are also *just parts*. The energy that we source through our bodies at the directives of and in harmony (or disharmony) with our souls. We name men and women for the masculine and feminine aspects because of the body's ability to perform within the functions of procreation.

But what do we want to BE? What energy does our soul most harmonize with? This is almost always a complex mix of elements, depending on who we are with and what we are trying to achieve. With so much in motion, it's easy to get lost in the vagueness of self-analyzing and identifying. But there's no reason to get lost. There are only a couple elements that actually need to be focused on to make a better life on this planet for ourselves and those we love.

1) Our Mind has to be Divine Masculine, in service of the Human Heart and the rest of the emotional body. This does not mean ONLY masculine, as Divine Masculine can and will shift and adjust if need be. That's the job. It will protect the heart from the perverted/juvenile masculine that resides in the Egoic Mind.

2) We have to be Divine Feminine when in Observation Consciousness, as it allows and respects all incoming information so that it can be used as an opportunity, not wasted.

3) We have to be the Divine Parent *that is needed for the situation*, rather than the one that is easiest or most convenient. This will get more explanation later on.

4) We can switch through all of these aspects of ourselves in a matter of SECONDS if we *commit* to *training ourselves to do so*.

The truth is that our nature and being, as well as the energies flowing through us, can and will change over our lives, but the ability to use certain tools and apply certain wisdom will take similar forms. This traces back to Jung's archetypes, of course, but is truly the embodiment of Myth in our daily lives. It is how we take the divine energy flowing within us, and make Synergy. It's more than just a language of expressing connection, but a never-ending font of realities sourcing from that commitment.

We become the Sun and Earth. We become Time and Space. We become Seed and Womb.

Chapter 4:

I Want More

I love relationships. I want more of them to flourish.

I started doing relationship therapy as a freshman in high school. I'm sure I'm not the only freshman to jump at the chance to talk to older girls who wanted to whine about their boyfriends, but it's likely that I was the only one that had an extensive background in family systems therapy. The issues I saw at that age and the issues that I see now are not that different. The main issues remain the same. We have basically no idea how to do anything at all when it comes to emotion. Basically, I'm saying the issue is *widespread and systemic emotional incompetence.*

It's not our fault, though. We haven't been taught. None of us exist in a vacuum and none of our core beliefs were modeled on self-generated realities (remember when you raised yourself? Oh, wait … we didn't.). We were taught. More often than not, we were taught wrongly, conflictingly, or in a grossly incomplete fashion. Generally, from what I've witnessed, it's all three in combination. We can pretty much count on that for the majority of human beings living today. That's not too hard to believe, is it?

Our society has built a vast technological world for safety and independent activity, but has done so very little for interdependent activity. **Interdependence** is a state of being that is empowered and mutually beneficial for two or more people in concert, characterized by conscious role fluidity and experimentation to meet the needs of those involved. That's right, I basically had to make the freaking word up because it doesn't exist in today's lexicon (I know I didn't make it up). This is NOT to be confused with co-dependence, which is built on role security and stagnation and is rarely beneficial for anyone. This is INTERDEPENDECE. It is the healthy version of connected living.

Hugs. Ouch!

"Can't we all just … get along?"

"NO! WE CAN'T! WE DON'T KNOW HOW!"

Ahhhh … the sad truth. Incompetence. It's so frustrating. I was having a conversation with a friend and came up with an analogy that I loved, so I'll share it.

The 1000 Missed Hugs Analogy.

The world can be characterized as a group of super lonely, super sad, blind, deaf, uncoordinated people wandering around in the dark in a building (really, I think that's pretty accurate given our inability to manage our moods and emotional realities).

They all want love and healthy physical contact. They are thirsting for it deeply and *have no way of communicating*. They have not been taught. They have not been shown anything about how to move around, either. Sounds like a recipe for good times, right?

So when two people get close to one another, they try to hug. Let's call them Kid A and Kid B, since they are likely young. They've never hugged before, or seen anyone hug, so they swing their arms wildly … one person hits the other in the face and they both fall over in pain. That's what our first relationships in this crazy world usually look like. These are at least authentic, making them much more honest and decent then most of the relationships that follow. Because after those first floundering moments, everyone has been hurt at least once, and is trying to make contact *without being hurt*.

So Kid B got walloped in the face and Kid A is gun-shy about hitting anyone in the face. Kid B puts a brace over her hurt face and goes back out into the world. Kid A tries to figure out a way to hug without using his arms.

The unfortunate way that works is that the next person each of them comes into contact with has to deal with whatever apparatus they are using to keep from being hurt. It's tough to make close contact with a brace over one's face, so Kid B has a layer of protection Kid C can't get through and either thinks it is their fault and becomes ridiculously frustrated. Kid A will not really embrace anyone so when he meets up with Kid D, Kid D becomes attention-starved and frustrated … and Kid A is just trying to protect them. This is all in combination with whatever issues Kids C and D have also.

This goes on forever … as each new relationship is working with the templates of past relationships, their barriers and resistance and anguish *being the defining reasons that the new relationships don't work*.

But why is all of this insanity the way it is?! Because we don't learn how to hug in the first place, and *after we fail we stop trying to learn*. We don't learn that it's difficult, but possible (which is the truth). It's not freaking magic. It's work.

It is focusing on learning how to give love and stop fearing pain, so that we can HONOR the love we feel and honor the desires within our hearts. That way, Kid A and Kid B can take off the braces and start learning how to move their arms, using more and more care and learning more and more technique.

Then, and only then, they have a chance at getting what they really want.

I want more. Not just more people connected healthily. Not just more languages of love being spilled into the collective. I want more EXCITEMENT. I want people *excited about engaging the insanity of other people* and knowing the unbelievable odds they are up against BEFORE going into a relationship. I want to feel the collective excitement at the opportunity to get our asses kicked trying to love another living being. I want excitement for all the misunderstandings, all the confusion, all the issues *that neither person caused* but that *both have to deal with*.

I want this to be exciting. I want the adventure *to be an adventure*.

Do you want that? I'm asking. Like, I'm really asking you, that's reading this book right now **… is that what you want**? You don't *HAVE* to want it. This chapter is about me telling you what I want. Me … telling YOU … *what I want*. You're not me. You may want something totally different. But there's something I know … what I want is possible to have. I know this because I have it. (It's also really fun, even though it takes some getting used to.)

Why do I mention that it's possible? Because much of what people want, from what I can see, is totally impossible. Not only that, but a great deal of what people want is not something that would make that someone happy even if they could have it. I do cover all of the specifics of how that issue unfolds throughout the rest of the book …

but the most common idea is that everyone seems to want something for nothing, or to have all the good stuff without working through any of the bad.

Besides being an obviously ridiculous thing to want, it exposes something about our cultural understanding of relationships. This is that we have a juvenile understanding of how to go about creating happiness, at best. At worst, we're toddlers.

Toddlers don't go on adventures, and juveniles are a burden on one.

I've mentioned that it's not our faults. It's not our parents' faults either. No one is at fault for evolution, and that's what we're dealing with. I'm not sure when the need for an evolving social structure started (though I have plenty of educated guesses), but the need has been neglected for generations now, leaving us in an odd gap. We exist in a time after the survival structure was enough … when women relied on men to protect them and finance them, and they'd raise the kids. And that was enough. They didn't have to be happy. Heck, they didn't even worry about being happy, for the most part. They just did what they were supposed to.

Then we got good at surviving. Then it wasn't enough to just survive. Then how happy we were (or how happy we were not, more commonly) started becoming an issue.

This is where we are now, and why my wants and attention on this issue matter to me so much. We don't really have a reason to just survive anymore. It's not good enough. We need some level of connection and joy that is meaningful, in order to keep the species going. For this, we need to have sophisticated and intimate relationships.

Where "avoiding pain and death" was enough for thousands of years, it simply no longer is. Grunt work without meaningful reward is not going to get it done. So, we HAVE to work our way into the ability to find and nourish soul connections and inspire others to do the same.

This is why I am writing this … to share with you my desire. To share with you why I believe it is vitally important for everyone. To share my excitement for each and every one of you as we move forward through an evolving world with more individual ecstasy and resonance as the very fuel the evolution depends on for sustenance.

I want more … and I want you to want it, too.

Chapter 5

... Co-Parenting the Self and the Divine Other

Interdependence is a goal. It's a goal because without it we will not ever have the safety to do what couples do best ... play. And what is the main component necessary for interdependence and play? The ability to PARENT.

This does not mean that we need to be critical or stressing about giving guidance and suggestions all day ... not at all. It REALLY does not mean we need to treat our partners like babies or micro-manage them. So let's take those ideas off the table immediately. Why? Because that's not *good* parenting. It's *bad* parenting. It doesn't promote growth or freedom, nor does it inspire trust. We need good Parenting in our relationships.

Parenting within a relationship is mainly about **Role Fluidity** and meeting each other's needs in a kind and supportive manner. Role Fluidity is the ability to shift perspectives and focus in such a way that our *momentary identity* and perspective aligns with what can be *most helpful* for the situation. I talk about this in Coffee for Consciousness 101 as being a main talent of the **New Archetype** (the archetype which contains and flows between all other archetypes consciously), and it is a vital understanding for engaging in Interdependence.

And remember the key word up there in italics ... "most helpful."

What can I do right now to be helpful?

Figuring out how to be helpful seems like a basic enough focus, but when we are in a heated and confusing moment with our significant other, the task becomes Herculean.

When we're the most hurt? *That is the time to be kind and gentle.*

When we're the most frustrated? *That is the time to be patient.*

When we're the most frightened? *That is the time to be courageous and clear-headed.*

When we're the most angered? *That is the time to be calm.*

When things look the worst? *That is the time to be hopeful and supportive.*

When there is trouble … *don't attack.* When there is an abandonment … *hold steady.* When there is fury … *remain non-reactive.* When there is doubt … *remain stable.* When there is guilt and shame and hurt … *don't indulge anger.* And when there is failure at any or all of these … *don't get lost in guilt and don't give up trying.* It's a tall SET of orders, not just a tall order.

Basically? What we would want to do with our child in the best circumstance? We try to do the same with our partners. Why? Because it works … and because **NOT DOING IT DOESN'T WORK**. Refusing to step into a Parenting role when it is needed … ***doesn't work***.

There is a ridiculous assumption upon entering adulthood that we are adults dealing with other adults, when in actuality, 99% of the time we are kids *impersonating what we think adults should be doing* and *dealing with others doing the same thing.*

We aren't adults. We're kids with briefcases and driver's licenses. Great impersonators. We haven't been taught to manage our emotions or conduct the internal majesty of our consciousness. We. Are. Still. Growing.

We all need more parenting. Period. Again ... WE ALL NEED MORE PARENTING.

The first question we need to ask ourselves is ...

"Am I willing to parent?"

This is a great question ... because when I was a kid, I thought I wouldn't have to do anything like that when I grew up. I thought adults were healthy sovereign beings that could self-manage. I don't think that now. I know now that I may have to take on a larger role to keep situations healthy and happy. So, before going into any situation, I have to ask myself if I'm ready to do that and WILLING to do that *if the need arises*. If I'm not feeling up to it? I don't go into the situation.

Second question.

"Am I willing to Parent **when it is needed**, rather than just *when it is convenient?*"

This is a major one, and it harkens back to a page ago when I was describing how hard it was to be parental when we're activated and upset. It not only demands that we step into a larger role with more responsibility ... but that we do it when we are not at our best.

Why must we do this, and how do we do it?

We must do it because it creates trust and intimacy and gives us the greatest opportunity for expansion and growth.

How we do it is by Self-Parenting first. Self-Parenting is primarily the practice of Processing Emotion in real time so that we are not dominated by destructive emotion when we need to be calm in order to take the opportunities we are presented with.

It comes down to housecleaning, actually. But the house is not just the 3D enclosure we dwell in, it's the **Relationship House**. The Relationship House is the symbolic representation of the connection between people that exists OUTSIDE of them, that they are beholden to take care of in order to keep the relationship healthy. When two people are IN a relationship, they are IN a third thing … that thing is the Relationship House.

This structure contains everything about the two people, all the messes and traumas and mistakes and dreams and blah blah blah … everything that comes with people. EVERYTHING.

In order for there to be play and joy, the house has to be decently clean. Why? *Because our inner children cannot play in a dirty environment*. Resentment, anger, frustration, confusion, etc.--all of these create a dangerous environment for inner children to play in. They are fragile, easily hurt, and *very difficult to reassure once damage has been done* to their confidence. This is why we have to have our inner parents on duty to make sure that the inner children have the room and safety they need. They need a safe environment.

For the Inner Child to come forward, there have to be trustworthy parents on duty.

We don't feel safe. This isn't weird, and honestly, it isn't even news. The inner child vocabulary has been around for at least thirty years now, and I expect most have heard it. But how we get at our inner child and why this is important can get lost in the rhetoric, psychobabble and spiritualized behavioral prescriptions doled out by the many different factions of people that are using the term.

So ... let's distill it so that we can use it. The inner child has our sweetest selves and our most passionate desires flowing through it. I often equate it to the Heart, but the inner child is not as sophisticated and not nearly as strong. The inner child is easily wounded, and as it has actually endured childhood, it is likely carrying around a TON of trauma and fear from being brutalized into growing up.

I'll say it again ... it is carrying fear from being BRUTALIZED into GROWING UP. This is a process we all go through. The pain and trauma are byproducts of growth in society. They are normal. While some have it to more or less of a degree, we all have it. That's okay. We want to be able to work with it, though, and as we look into the eyes of the person we love, we want to be able to coax their inner child out so that we can play with them. That's what love seems to be most joyously striving toward, in my experience.

But how do we coax the sweet child in our lover out when they are scared to death of being hurt? This is a question that needs to be asked, and the answer, from what I've seen, is pretty basic. When they NEED us to be there to parent them through fear, WE SHOW UP..

When the trauma from childhood, or an old relationship, or even random phobias attack them and put them in a state of resistance and fear, we show up as parents. We show up AS NEEDED. We show up WITHOUT RESENTMENT, WITHOUT COMPLAINT, and WITHOUT RIDICULE.

If we miss any one of those components, **we lose the trust of our partner's inner child, and resentment begins to build within them toward us**. That's the truth, there's no way around it, and there's nothing we OR our partner can do to stop it. That's the nature of our inner children. They don't need to ever come out. They don't owe it to anyone. They have no need to forgive, and no one can make them do something they don't want to do. They can just hide forever. No skin off their back. Dealing with inner children is an exercise in HOPE. It demands the best of what we have to offer just to get the process going. Coaxing an inner child forward is a long process, even with the most courageous people. Without being able to show up and Parent each other, it's not going to work. It's just not.

There are a couple more aspects I want to get into about Parenting in relationships, because it's confusing when we have to analyze and dig without knowing exactly what we're looking for.

The first of these aspects has to do with what Parenting commonly looks like when it's difficult.

What we are probably going to have to do …

I say "probably" because it's not certain what form our parenting will take, as each person is different and how we self-parent makes different aspects of these many "possible" tasks more difficult. But the *primary* thing we are looking for to stimulate us into a larger perspective is DISTRESS.

Distress is our opportunity.

When we are with our own children and just walking along, we don't have to start parenting until our youngster falls down or gets grumpy. Then we are stimulated into a larger perspective so that we can tend to our child's needs. This is all about Opportunity.

When distress comes forward through our significant others or our friends, we tend to their needs so that they can help process what they are going through (whether they are actually doing that, or just transferring anger or frustration, is another conversation). We show up. We listen. We ascertain what the nature of the distress is and we respond in a way that will help them (rather than in a way we think they should respond favorably to--HUGE difference).

The two MAIN manners in which this happens between men and women are going to be showcased below. There are many others, and these are NOT gender-specific, just gender "probable" ... okay?

Daddy-Daughter tantrum ...

In the role of the masculine attending to a female reaction of distress, it's much like a father attending to the needs of a young girl in an emotionally volatile state. Women can throw tantrums just like little girls, and they are often much more frightening (men throw tantrums too, don't worry). But these are normal.

There are many who would say that they're not normal and need to be controlled. I have never seen that work out. I've seen it lead to repression and resentment, though, so if that's what you're looking for, by all means go for that tactic.

If a man wants to be there for his significant other when

she is in distress, he has to take it the same way a good father would if his daughter was going ballistic.

How do we do this? We take her distress seriously. We may be able to see totally clearly that there is not an issue *in the world* that corresponds to what she's feeling, but it doesn't matter. Why? Because the issue is not in the world, it is *IN HER BODY*. Only after it gets internally managed does she have a chance at returning to a relaxed state (and she will return to a relaxed state, trust that).

If a woman wants to be there for her man when he is in distress, she has to do it the way a good mother would if her son was losing it.

How does a woman do this? She recognizes that her man is trapped focusing on something that is swallowing him and making him want to run away. It's real to him. Whatever failure or stressor is crushing him, it's real. But it's not the only thing in the world and it's not the final thing in his life. So we as women do what a good mother would do after her son had a hard time with something … we remind him that his effort is the primary focus, that the failure is not his last chance, and that we have faith in him no matter what because he is a good person.

Men show up and withstand the temporary emotional tantrum, women show up and redirect male frustration and provide support and confidence. That's it. It's not complex, but it's pretty difficult to do if we are caught off guard *or have no idea what we are supposed to be doing*. It's impossible if we think that we're not supposed to have to parent our significant others. We just won't do it. And each time we miss an opportunity? The relationship gets more and more distant, and the two people in it get more and more frightened, leading to the inner children shrinking off into the distance, never to be seen again.

The next aspect I want to talk about has been driven by the questions I've received in my decades of giving relationship advice, and it's not easy to take.

The Parenting Isn't EQUAL!!

Really? Equal?

Many people wonder how much parenting one SHOULD do. What if one person parents more than the other? What if the percentage is like 90-10? 75-25?

So I'll say it again.

WE. PARENT. WHEN. NEEDED.

If we don't want to? If it's too much? If we don't like how one-sided it is? If we aren't getting Parented when we need it? WE LEAVE. We don't complain, and we don't use a perceived lack of Parenting on someone else's part to justify our not partaking in doing our part when we're needed.

We never pass up an opportunity to Parent if we see it. That's the job of being in a relationship. When people say, "Relationships are hard work," this is the work they are talking about. If we don't want to do it? We're not going to be in a good relationship. That's fine too; we just better not complain, because that is disingenuous and will sap our integrity from our body.

Can we ask for help? Of course. But we sign up for Parenting when we get involved with another person, whether we know it or not, whether we agree to it or not. Allowing that truth to exist *and dealing with it,* rather than pretending it doesn't exist, will save everyone a lot of time and energy. And both time and energy are beyond valuable if happiness is something we want to have.

It's a lot. I know. It's a lot to not worry about whether or not it's fair. It's a lot to stimulate ourselves into Parenting when we're upset. It's a lot of pressure to realize that we need to do it whenever the opportunity arises. It's also a lot to know we're going to mess up and that we're not going to be able to succeed every time. It's a lot to know that the health and happiness of the relationship is going to depend on it. It's all a lot.

But … it's realllllly worth it.

It's worth it when we show up for someone and it works. It's worth it when we get closer and closer, and trust builds. It's worth it when we're in a terrible situation and we have undying faith that it's temporary because all distress is temporary when there are willing parents to clean up the mess. It's worth it when intimacy is DEEP because both people know in their heart that they have shown up for each other (this is really rare and really powerful in a way that nothing else is). It's worth it when horrific things happen and the bond is unshakeable. It's worth it when shame and fear before our mates is not even something we can imagine anymore. It's worth it when we know if we lose ourselves completely, we will have help pulling ourselves back together.

And it's really worth it to know that when our partner needs anything … they will be coming to US. Every time. Because WE are the person they need.

If you want to trade that in for ease and comfort, be my damn guest. I wouldn't trade it for anything in the world. Not. A. Thing.

Chapter 6:

Prime Issues: The Addendum to Parenting

This chapter could have been tacked on to the Parenting chapter, but given how specific its focus is going to be, I figured it best to set it apart.

There are Prime Issues the Masculine and Feminine face that most major issues stem from. We can most easily see this with men and women, but it is really the masculine and feminine ... regardless of gender. It also occurs *WITHIN all of us* and I will outline the internal and external struggles as we ALL should know them inside and out, backwards and forwards. That is IF we want to achieve harmony and happiness. IF.

The Prime Issue for the Feminine is abandonment. The Prime Issue for the Masculine is Wasted Energy. These are Prime issues *as I have found them*, NOT THE ONLY ISSUES.

Let's take a moment to imagine. Pull yourself back to a view of the solar system ...

Imagine if the Sun stopped shining? (All life on Earth dies.)

Imagine if the Earth turned away from the Sun and stopped producing life, became lifeless while basking in its light? (All the Sun's energy is wasted.)

The analogies with cosmic bodies seem to be poignant, don't they? Doesn't each of those situations seem tragic and powerful? Don't they hurt to think of? Looking at these examples makes it easier to see how much damage can be done when we engage in this here within our own lives. This is the moment we bring the mythic and obvious down from the heavens and ground it in our daily lives.

These issues come with the incarnation into physical bodies on this Earth plane, and fall under what I will describe in more detail later, **Biological Imperatives**. Biological Imperatives are built into our DNA to make sure the species survives, and as we have not come out of caves until the last 100-200 thousand years, they are still deeply embedded in our motivational matrices.

Breaking Down the Biological Imperative

Man: "I can't build a baby to continue my genetic line. I'm at your mercy for that. I'll give you all my energy, will you build me a person?"

Woman: "I can build a person, but it makes me vulnerable forever, and I can't protect myself in a vulnerable state. You're going to hang around and make sure a tiger doesn't eat me, right?"

The basis of Masculine/Feminine synergy exists within making this deal. Neither one of them can do it on their own. The drive to do so is powerful, and the survival of the species depends on it. Biological Imperatives are not to be argued with. They are to be accepted, integrated, and overcome if necessary. That's a big IF. It's generally not necessary to overcome them; just understanding them is enough.

Mind: "Hey, you have desires built in to you. You naturally seek connections and expansion. I like that and can't generate that on my own. If you keep talking to me about what you want, I may be able to make it happen, and we'll both be happy."

Heart: "I have desires but so little power in the human body. You basically run the whole thing, and I am at your mercy to honor me and move forward toward my desire with our mutual best interest in mind. But I can promise you, I'll reward you with great emotional experience if you listen to me."

Both scenarios lead to synergy. Man and woman … mind and heart. There is no family or language without them working together, and BOTH are ALWAYS NATURALLY FRIGHTENED *that the other one is not going to do their part*.

The basis of our Prime Issues is that we have needs and we cannot control how things are going to play out. That is horrific to us as sentient beings. Remember group work in middle school? This is much, much scarier.

We are trying to build harmony within ourselves for resonance, and we are trying to build a family outside of ourselves for posterity, and NEITHER is fully within our control. Our mind has to trust our heart, and human beings have to trust each other. That. Is. Horrifying.

Looking at the Masculine side and the Feminine side individually will show us how justified our fears are. This does not mean, in any way, that we are going to allow them to stop us. This only means that we are going to humbly respect their presence and power within us so that we can manage their presence effectively. They were there to ensure that our partners gave our genetics the best chance at survival, and honestly, that's still the case.

"Don't waste my energy, please" says the masculine.

It's all we have as men. We have the structures we produce that prove how strong we are, and we have our muscles, literal and figurative. But without someone and something to protect and fuel, we are basically empty of purpose.

In the same way, the mind only has organization, logic, analysis, and the ability to translate. When the heart doesn't use it to organize its creations, the mind is basically pointless.

"All we have is our time, energy, logic, money, house, car, strength, power, and care … if those are wasted, our lives will be wasted."

What's the worst feeling? The worst ever for men? It's when we give everything to our mate, and she isn't happy. It's not enough. What do we think to ourselves? "Well then why did I do ANY OF THIS?! IT WAS A WASTE!"

The mind says the same thing when the heart gets broken. The mind tries to give its all to the heart's purposes, and can come up empty … it happens often.

Of course, it's not true. *There's no such thing as wasted experience.* Wasted time? Wasted life? *It does not exist.* All experiences build our fortitude and foundation, as well as providing us with character in the present moment. But, we don't know that intrinsically. We have to come to understand that everything in relationships is a process, rather than the end-all-be-all of existence. It's actually why people common-ly say "Hey, it's not the end of the world" to people who have been hurt. They say it because when we are deeply injured, it DOES feel like it is the end of the world (especially the first fifty or so times).

Every rejection is a trauma. It becomes a statement about a man's existence that we are not enough, that everything we have done has been wasted. Take a moment, whether you are a man or woman, and *feel that desperate mourning for every rejection in history*. I know that sometimes it is curious and crazy how hard men take rejection … but it shouldn't be. If we are not accepted, in many ways we don't exist. Just empa-thize with that for a moment. This is why there is horror, and why much of what men do is tentative (especially if we are caring people). We have tried to build an existence, a reality that CANNOT BE TAKEN away. But it can, simply by being rejected. Men slowly realize, if they are strong, that they must accept themselves on their own terms. But we must see, as a society, how powerful this initial programming is and how difficult it is to overcome.

Women, in this case, can see both sides of this issue (which is an empathic advantage) because they too have struggles between their minds and their hearts. They too can feel the crushing pain of having given all with their mind, and had it not work out.

Unfortunately, men are at a deep disadvantage in under-standing women, because as a survival-focused society, we have not been allowing our hearts to the forefront (much less leading with them, as we should be).

So for men, while they can see wasted energy, wasted time, wasted money, and wasted production very clearly …

they cannot see the issues of the Feminine, again putting them at an even deeper disadvantage when it comes to bridging the gaps of communication and understanding between the masculine and feminine.

Show up. Stay Present. Simple directions that are really hard to follow. Women say it to men, and the human heart says it to the mind. The mind and the man can both say "Of course, that's all you need? That's not hard" and then be *running a million miles an hour out the door* ten minutes later.

Why is this such an issue? It is an issue because the woman and the heart both sacrifice their body and safety to try to create new connections and realities. They put themselves in a vulnerable state to create life, and to honor them we must not make them face that alone. That is all they ask ….

Abandonment Issues

Women share. It's the nature of the female body. It's a beautiful thing. That's why matriarchal societies are built on sharing rather than female dominance, unlike patriarchies (which are built on competition and dominance). Women live in everything they touch, and expand into their world in a glorious and intimate way.

But, ummmmmm, that doesn't mean it's fun. That doesn't mean there aren't serious difficulties associated with being the gender that bears children. That doesn't mean there aren't marked differences that create serious confusion between the sexes when they are not recognized and HONORED.

What do women "generally" have that needs to be honored?

Weaker bodies (less muscle mass, less testosterone, 10% less height and 30% less weight).

Heightened emotions and impulsivity.

Heightened bonding depths.

Bodies that undergo destabilizing changes every twenty-eight days.

Bodies that are at risk of becoming impregnated.

The state of pregnancy itself, which lasts nine months and has a destructive and beautiful effect on the body.

Bodies that are deemed attractive BEFORE childbearing years, rather than after.

Bodies that are "perceived" to decline with age and usage.

Fear of having any of the above used to take advantage of them.

Heightened vulnerability at all stages of life.

I am an empath and have been studying human behavior since I was a boy. Now, as a man, I cannot imagine what it's like to live with all of that. Do I consider them disadvantages in and of themselves? NO. Of course not. They are the reason I have such respect for women and recognize what deep strength women possess.

In order to raise a family with a man, women have to give up even more. Time, freedom, beauty, YOUTH. They give up things they can NEVER get back.

We're different, men and women. I also recognize that all human beings are different. The way that we are equal is in how we HONOR those differences, not in how we PRETEND THEY DON'T EXIST. So, in this book, we're not going to pretend.

Women have abandonment issues because they have to give something up in the reproduction process. They give up things that are valuable to them. A woman can't "walk away" from a pregnancy any more than she can decide to not menstruate. She's vulnerable.

And that ends up being the whole thing. Abandonment issues aren't *issues* at all. They are Darwinian structures built in to ensure the highest likelihood of stability for the self and the incoming child. They are ANTI- ABANDONMENT PROGRAMS ... not *issues*.

Women live in fear of being bailed on by their partners because their partners CAN LEAVE. Women can't leave their own bodies. They can't walk away.

So, deeply in every woman's body there is a program running to push men away ... why? Because if they go when it's not that difficult? They're definitely going to bail when it gets really hard. And it ALWAYS gets really hard. I can't highlight this fact enough.

This raises a question: "If it's a part of natural selection, why must it be overcome?"

That's a good question. The answer is simple: "*Because we want to run the program rather than the program running us.*" Women want to know when they're testing someone, and that their level of testing isn't based on faulty programming or undermining self-sabotage. Because "Just how much pushing is a good thing? How much is the right amount?"

We can't know. We can't. Everyone is different.

Relationships for me are about recognizing the infinite differences and HONORING THEM. That's where equality lies for me, the *ability of one person to honor another*. When everyone can deeply honor each other's differences, we will have a world of equality. Not before. That is the path we, as a species, have been denying for a long time. It's time to stop. It's time to learn our differences and find the justice and equality in honoring those differences.

Chapter 7:

#RelationshipGoals

In writing this book, I am assuming a lot. I am assuming that people want intimacy and the challenge of closeness, and that they are willing to stretch their comfort zones *and work* in order to get it.

I am assuming that many want to know all the ways of moving forward, *not just the easy ones*. I am assuming that part of what people are wanting is to embrace a glorious challenge. I am assuming that many are willing to call themselves out on their own bullshit and investigate their actual motivations. I am assuming that many people aren't worrying about whether or not the relationship is equal, only that THEY KNOW THEY GAVE IT EVERYTHING FROM THEIR END. I am assuming that many people are willing to get hurt in order to form deep connections. I am assuming that many people are excited to try to BE the person they would want to be with, rather than just excited to FIND the person they would want to be with. I am assuming *a lot*.

If you are reading this, *I am assuming it of you*.

We need to work because what we are capable of receiving in a relationship relates directly to what we are capable of giving and how much effort and risk we are capable of engaging in. The whole "You get what you give" cliché has a foundation in practical psychology. Someone who cheats to win gets the trophy but doesn't get the sense of victory. You can't get that when you cheat. So in writing this, I am assuming that there are a lot of people who want to EARN their blessings in the land of love. Because that's what we're talking about. Earning Blessings.

Being free of Resentment. Developing our internal desire in such a way that it includes the *whole of the person* we are desiring and their personal growth. Being committed to working together as new challenges arise. Then finally, an enduring depth of intimacy from endless digging.

These are Relationship Goals as I see them. I'm assuming you want these.

One blessing, likely the most important, is being free of resentment toward those we are in relationships with (as well as those we *have been* in relationships with). Resentment is the most common psychological brutality we live with, and its poison can dominate our reality very easily. It is the worst possible result of any connection, and from what I've seen, it is also the most common. The prevention of resentment is my most important Relationship Goal.

Resentment Is Death

"What's the worst that could happen?"

"Resentment. I could go from loving you to hating you."

My main relationship goal is *not allowing that to happen*. Everything else can be worked with. The worst thing is not pain and loss, not rejection, not betrayal, but that the love I feel within me and the image of the person I care for can be so twisted by anger *that the beauty that once existed in my heart turns to hate*. That is the death of the relationship. It is the death of beauty. It is the death of love within us. It is the death of the Divine Other.

We commit to working within relationships so that this doesn't happen. The only way this happens is if we LET IT HAPPEN. Other people don't create resentment within us ... we LET IT HAPPEN through our inattention to its presence and our inaction.

How do we let resentment happen? What is the mechanism by which it occurs?

It's simple. Whatever weaknesses we have are reflected back to us through our partner, and we *blame them* for the way *we end up feeling about ourselves*.

The tough part is that we do not go into any relationship knowing what *all* of our weaknesses are, much less having a healthy relationship with them. We barely know ourselves, and now we're trying to know someone else. Often, these unknown weaknesses get found IN THE PROCESS of being in a relationship and we are caught off guard (in fact, *I'd say this is a guarantee*). If we cannot stomach being shown our own weaknesses because of how they conflict with our picture of ourselves, then we become resistant to doing what is needed to heal the anger that we are feeling toward ourselves.

We feel betrayed by our expectations of who we believed ourselves to be, and we SHUT DOWN **rather than accepting the opportunity to adjust our view of ourselves** to incorporate the new information. This creates a huge amount of anger and distress within us that we are unlikely to process healthily.

Whatever anger lingers within us and is not healed, it becomes targeted at the person who allowed us to see our weakness. **That is how resentment happens**. Now that we know, we can commit ourselves to stopping it. We don't resent the ones we love for their weaknesses. We resent them for **ours**.

One of my best examples of this happened with my young-est stepson. I have been focusing on not allowing myself to step into states of resentment my whole life, so as I had this experience with him I could maneuver and process healthily to ensure I wouldn't resent him for what he showed me about myself. I also think it's powerful to see how this works with a child, because of how much differently we treat adults … adults that we also have to spend time parenting.

What he showed me about myself? I wasn't very good with new technology. Big surprise.

It was only my second or third time being alone with him and his brother, and I was leaning pretty heavily on gumption and confidence to get the whole "adulting" thing down. Then I had to figure out the TV remote. I had to switch from regular programming to some newfangled gaming station. I looked confused at the odd remote device in my hands and then told my youngest that he had to wait a moment while I asked his older brother how to work it.

He looked stunned, and said, "You're an adult and you don't know how to work a TV?" … yeah. I got my ass handed to me by a seven-year-old. Now my mind went straight to "Hey! I know TVs just fine I just haven't learned about this stupid TV because I don't watch TV and think you shouldn't be gaming that much anyway! What the hell!?"

But I didn't say that. Not just because it would have been really nasty and unwise, given my love for him and his moth-er. But I didn't say it because he had just shown me a weak-ness in myself, and I wasn't mad at him AT ALL. I was mad at myself. I was mad that I wasn't more prepared to be a father. Why on Earth would an insult from a seven-year-old both-er me? Because I was scared. Unprepared. I was winging it and *he totally nailed me*. I was found out, and SHOWN MY WEAKNESS.

That is how resentment happens. We feel weak based on something external to us and we find a target to assign blame for our bad feelings. That target is now the object of our animosity and held anger. As long as that anger is dominating our consciousness, the love we feel for the target now lessens, because anger undermines their beauty in our eyes.

That sucks. It just does. But this is what we do in relationships. This is a certainty in most relationships ... and for some unknown reason, we don't seem to care that much if it occurs and destroys everything. It could be the most poisonous thing to a relationship, and we are not even aware of when it is happening. That is obscene and unnecessary.

The big question I ask myself is "HOW DARE I?"

That's the question I like to pose myself each time I allow resentment or anger to creep into my reality for even a second. How. Dare. I?

How dare I tarnish the beautiful blooming of desire within my heart with anger? How dare I tarnish my image of my love, my child, or my friend with the rotting garbage that is resentment? How dare I allow whatever weakness I may be embarrassed of to USURP my HONOR and allow me to stash nasty feelings toward another IN OPPOSITION TO MY HEART?

I know of no uglier thing in this world than resentment (have I made that abundantly clear yet?). It is the expression of cowardice and impotence run amok in the world through our body with or without our conscious consent. It is, quite simply, allowing ourselves to be possessed by the worst parts of our nature in such a way that *we demonize what we most deeply love*.

This ends up being our primary relationships. Our mates, our children, our friends, our coworkers. They end up being the target for our **Anger Transference**, and the initial movement to attack becomes a *permanent division* that has to be further justified by **Mental Instinct** (The egoic need to justify our feelings by cherry-picking information to support it).

I've been going pretty hard at it, and I think I've gotten my overall "resentment bad" point across. But while I hinted at what a resentment-expressive moment would be like with my youngest, I have not done one with my Mate. The cool thing is, I'm not going to do a big one ... I'm going to show off a little one. I'm doing this to show just how powerful, subtle, and seductive they are.

So, tonight, before typing this, I was taking the garbage out. The garbage was overfilled. I had to get out another bag and dump the whole thing upside down in the large can outside. Oh! The humanity! Just a minor occurrence on an average day, not even something that cost me more than an extra three minutes' work. But I could blame her. If there was any part of me that was holding on to anger about anything? I could have gone on a mini tirade in my head about how "she can't be all pushing the garbage down and has to be more careful about the bagging and should have let me know how full it was earlier." That's three avenues I could have taken to allow resentment into my field. Why was the inspiration even there, though?

It was there because I was *actually* mad at myself because I hadn't checked to see how full the garbage can was ... because *I wasn't paying attention to the stuff I need to* as a parent and husband. I was EMBARRASSED and angry at myself, and so *my mind* NATURALLY STARTED TO TAKE IT OUT ON HER. That.

Seriously. Just. Happened. I'm still sweating from being out in the humidity as I type. I was mad at myself, so I went to attack her in my mind. This is a natural habit of consciousness, and it happens so often that I'm surprised relationships last as long as they do. If I was in a less conscious or worse mood? I would have let myself get away with it. So I'm gonna say it again …

HOW DARE I?

We should all be prepared to say it to ourselves the second we get into a relationship, and prepared to say it FOREVER to ourselves to PROTECT that relationship.

Seriously. Call yourself out. It'll change your life, and it'll make your relationship with everyone stronger than it has ever been.

The biggest reason that resentment is so prevalent is that we get more than we bargained for, and in general we are incapable of handling it. When we form Primary relationships, whether consciously or unconsciously, we are inviting the whole of another human being into our "space" (Relationship House). Naturally, we would prefer to pick and choose which aspects of our Divine Partner get allowed into the Relationship House, and we may even think we can do that. But we can't. That's "CAN'T." It's **Impossible**.

So what do we need to be saying to ourselves as we go into these relationships? I can only be sure about what I said about Claudia.

"I want ALL OF HER. ALL."

The Whole Mess

Do you want ALL of someone? You think you're up for the challenge? Do you want someone to want ALL of YOU? Or are we dealing with "just the positive" … or "the best parts of their nature as we see it"? Do we have any idea what it means to want all of someone? Are we prepared to have someone want all of us?

The "Whole Mess" of a human being is no joke. It's bottomless. It's overwhelming. It's also what we sign up for when we enter into a relationship, regardless of what level of consciousness created the relationship. Getting the Whole Mess isn't an option. It's the foundation. The only options we have lie in how we want to try to navigate the mess once we're in it … and *how we approach the mess* when we initially engage it.

We have to want it. We have to want the whole damn thing. That's the only way we're going to have the energy to face it without getting resentful. "In sickness and in health?" … yeah, that's the understatement of the millennium.

When we form a bond with anyone, we allow for a decent amount of "mess" crossover.

When we form a Primary Bond? We get every trauma, every ex, every illness, every phobia, every pet peeve, every moment of abuse, every past life and bit of karmic debt (if you're into that sort of deliciousness), every hope, every dream, every shame, every obsession, everything, everything, everything. We humans are a MESS.

When we form friendships, there are generally boundaries and space that can be put comfortably in place … and even adjusted for comfort. When we form Primary Relationships …

we are trapped. We have to want to be trapped, in a mess, for-ever, with the person we choose to form a relationship with. Wanting that, welcoming it, embracing the opportunity, even *being honored by it* … that is a #RelationshipGoal.

If we start out understanding this and embracing it, then we have a shot at dealing with the huge amount of chaos that we are going to encounter within our Divine Other. What kind of chaos am I talking about?

If our Divine Other got teased in middle school? We have to deal with it.

If our Divine Other was abused? We have to deal with it.

If our Divine Other was traumatized by any one of a mil-lion things? We have to deal with it.

If our Divine Other has allergies? We have to deal with it.

If our Divine Other snores or has nightmares? We have to deal with it.

If our Divine Other has PTSD and severe anxiety (like me)? We have to deal with it.

If our Divine Other is predisposed to certain illnesses? We have to deal with it.

If our Divine Other is a _____ (insert their astrological sign, religion, addiction, ethnicity)? We have to deal with it.

If WE have any of these things? We have to be somewhat okay that *our Divine Other is going to have to deal with us, too*. That's a nasty little subtlety that often gets lost in the wash.

These aren't "options," these are simply part of the pack-age. They exist in the Relationship House, and if they are not properly attended to *they can damage it*, or *cause us to dam-age it by our reactivity* to them.

Those listed above are just the individual-specific ones. There are aspects of aging and physical changes in virility and health that occur with every single human being, and THOSE are ALSO difficult to deal with. And rarely do we go into a relationship thinking "Man, I'm gonna love changing their bedpan when they're eighty," … or "You're the one I want to watch me deteriorate and die."

That doesn't seem sexy. ***But it is***.

When we can step into the deep desire of another human being in such a way that it includes the WHOLE of their story, the amount of passionate energy we allow to flow through us meets NO RESISTANCE. When there is no resistance from fear or doubt, the fullness of our vitality can engage our drives for intimacy and deep connection. Sexy, indeed.

Now that we know that wanting to move forward into these messy areas is the ideal attitude, what is the next step? We don't start this immediately. But it's not far off … certainly not so far off that it's covered for the first time in the wedding vows.

It happens naturally. We naturally start to "see" more of someone the closer we get. When they start telling us about their day, when they start venting about issues they have with their family, when they complain about their boss. That's when the team-building-relationship-exercises begin and the emotional reality tests happen.

How do they respond to my venting and worry? How do I respond to theirs?

How is my mood affected by the way they speak? How is theirs affected by the way I speak?

How much does their mood and behavior fluctuate? Can I handle it? How much do my fluctuations affect them?

How do they handle problems? How frustrated do they get? Are they fun to work with? Am I?

How aware are they of their behavior? Can their self-awareness be challenged? Do they challenge mine in a way that works for me?

These are all vital questions that begin to form a picture of what the work will look like in the Relationship House. This is not what the work will be focused on (that can be anything, honestly), just *what it will look like* as the Divine Pair goes about tending the Relationship House as wear, tear, and discovery take place.

After we consciously assess these questions, and consciously discuss the mutual compatibility with our Divine Other, we really have only two questions to ask in order to move forward ...

Are you sure you want to do this?

How are we going to do this?

Wear, Tear, and Discovery ... the Nature of Endless Digging

People say a relationship is work. They're right. But the work is so specified to the couple and their goals, dreams, and temperaments that descriptions beyond that are difficult to come by. Also, much of the work comes from sustaining intimacy, and both parties have to want to do that **for the work to even present itself** within the relationship.

I said that accurately ... "for the work to present itself." *We don't get to choose what the work is or when it's going to show up.* We get to try to be ready and keep ourselves managed, then engage it as a couple the best we can while it is directly affecting us. This can be ultra-infuriating for those who are more given to planning and controlling circumstances.

This is why we want to ask, "Are you sure you want to do this?"

It might seem odd. It might seem like we're doubting or accusing our partner of wishy-washiness. But when your partner looks back at you and says, "You bet your ass. It's exactly what I want to be doing." Then we get something … and that something matters.

What we get is a full body and verbal representation of their devotion to the Mess. Also, when we give someone a way out and they don't take it, it reminds us that we have made a commitment, too. That is an invigorating moment. Being connected to someone who doesn't back down from a challenge is inspiring. That inspiration alone *can keep intimacy at high levels for the duration of a relationship.*

So ask. And know that you may be asked. It's not about doubting our partners, it's about *having humility* before the difficulties that we are all going to face.

The other question we are asking is "How are we going to do this?"

This may seem like a case-by-case issue as problems arise, but that is not how I am intending it. I am asking *"How are we going to approach problems?"* This is not as fluid as our actual strategies for problem-by-problem engagement.

There are specific ways that Claudia deals with my PTSD, my addiction issues, my anxiety, etc. But initially when we started to work with each other, she made it clear that she was going to work thoroughly, confidently, elegantly, and with a positive attitude. That's just how she *works*. I learned that by experiencing it and coming to trust it. This is the same way she learned how I work.

The thing that we learned about each other that drew us close, the thing that helps us stay connected and inspired, **is that we are always working**. We do it because we like it. We want everything to be better. We wake up creating and refining and we create and refine our way through the day. We enjoy it and we feed off each other's energy and creativity like an alternator recharging a car battery while it's in use.

That is how WE do it.

You are trying to find out how YOU do it. And this is not the singular "you" … this is "*you as a couple*." Because the way you do it with one person is NOT GOING TO BE THE SAME as when you do it with another. No two Relationship Houses are built the same, and no two people have the same garage full of junk (meant to type garbage, but I'll leave the typo, as it is a house feature). So no "How-to" is going to be the same. For that matter, the "How-to" is going to change during the course of every relationship. It changes because of wear and tear, and endless discovery.

The wear and tear and the endless discovery that exist in healthy relationships (and life, honestly) make these questions not only important to ask at the outset of a relationship, but for the duration of the relationship. That is what keeps the relationship alive.

The goals in this chapter are my goals. Honestly, even though it's not really my business, they are my goals for you to achieve, too. I have come to see that these are my goals over years of working with people and having my own experiences … they were not something I decided on. I can assure you that when I was young enough to think my decisions mattered, the decisions I made ended up not reflecting anything I cared about in relationships.

There is a good chance that you have made decisions about what your goals are, and that's awesome! I hope they work out better than mine did for me (like, not at all). But most importantly, I want you to observe what goals you develop during your life by watching closely your relationships and the relationships of others, because the internal and external worlds are ALWAYS CHANGING. And the only way to keep stride with change is to observe and adjust … observe and adjust ….

Maybe your goals will be like mine; maybe they won't. Mine aren't a bad place to start, though; they tend to lean towards kindness and authenticity. That's a good thing "pretty often" at the very least.

Chapter 8:

The Cave You Fear

There is a certain part about the masculine and feminine embracing each other that will always contain a deep fear. It is a natural fear … the one created when individuality exists … the one created when we are looking at an "other" outside of ourselves and wanting to make a connection.

Whether this is dealing with the search for an external Divine Union or the creation of an Internal Divine Union matters not. The connection itself contains a "fear" of *the other*. The *deeper* and *more intense* and *intimate* we want this connection to be, the more fear is generally going to be associated with it.

But it's worth it. It's worth it not just because we get to reap the rewards of close intimate connection, but because facing fear *is a treasure in and of itself.*

"The cave you fear holds the treasure you seek." --Joseph Campbell.

I've always lived/loved that quote. But for years I didn't understand it fully.

I kept thinking the treasure was something I wanted/would receive ON THE OTHER SIDE OF FEAR. I kept thinking "face the fear, get the reward".... But it's not that at all.

After I had lost my way and there was nothing I really wanted, I STILL had to face the fear. It didn't go away just because I was no longer searching. I was not a knight on a quest anymore, and now I had to face fear *just to get through everyday things*.

WHAT IS THAT ABOUT?!

Later I realized ... The treasure I was seeking? The treasure we all seek? ... IS THE ABILITY TO FACE, ENGAGE, and MANAGE fear.

THAT'S THE TREASURE. *That's why the fear we need to face doesn't go away*. The fear IS the quest of the Warriors and Knights of our time. The ability to engage it, harness it, manage it, embrace it, and transmute it *into courage* within us is the goal.

The only way to do that is to *allow ourselves to be uncomfortable* ... to stay PRESENT in the face of fear and discomfort "as much as we can."

Does this mean we let ourselves be brutalized? No. That's silly.

It means we find where the edge of our comfort zone is ... and we start stepping out of it.

This means, more than anything, **staying present with emotional reactions within ourselves that are uncomfortable**. It means trying to embrace the chaos of the heart rather than resisting it.

So much of this world makes us uncomfortable. The discomfort of a soul being in human form is not trivial. It is powerful and ever present. Thus ...

...the actual treasure *is not in the cave* ... it is the *willingness to keep going into caves*.

This relationship to fear becomes more and more important as we get to the deeper layers of intimacy in relationships ... the Mommy issues, the Daddy issues, abuse/trauma, and unspoken desires. The journey from "familiar stranger" (as all love interests seem to be) to Divine Union is less like a walk in the park and more like a walk *into a volcano while wearing a gasoline suit*. Taking seriously the difficulties that present themselves is a main focus of this book, so I'll likely get a little repetitive with them.

For the part of us that seeks to uncover the deep mysteries of the Divine Other, we are using the trailblazing part of our spirits. For the part that must accept what is found, we use the feminine aspect. So, in order to describe the mythic nature of how this takes place, I am going to use "knight and maiden" ... though it is really about "knight energy" in searching and "mother energy" when we make our discoveries.

Briar Patches and Metal Domes ...
Good Freaking Luck

Pretend each human soul is a maiden guarding a kingdom under a thicket of weeds and brush. Visualize it. This is the truth. Feel it. Feel the soul of the person you desire behind layers of weeds and brambles.

The maiden is calling a knight toward the thicket. No matter who we are, we are always calling someone. That is the nature of soul energy flowing through a human body. Regardless of whether we want it or not, we are always a match for something. The knight we are calling doesn't know what's under the brush. It could be gold, treasure, riches. So, he runs to the rescue of the maiden who is offering her kingdom.

But, when he gets there, it turns out that after pulling the brush away that there is a six-foot steel wall and dome over the entire area.

The maiden feels she's done her part to draw him close. We all feel this. We all feel like we put ourselves out there *enough*. If someone hits the real barriers to deeper intimacy and leaves ... we feel deeply abandoned. The knight who found the wall and was intimidated and left feels like he was *misled about the actual task* he was presented with. He feels betrayed. Both are injured. Both sides are right and both sides are wrong. This is how it happens when we're young for certain, and for as long into our adulthood as it takes to realize that *this is the BEGINNING of intimacy, not a block to it.*

My mate was unbelievably inviting, kind, and welcoming. When I pulled back the brush, there was a huge steel door. What to do?

I looked at her, smiled, and pulled out a key and unlocked it. Inside that there was a cement wall, and I broke it down. At each new level of intimacy, she freaked out ... but she freaked out less and less each time it happened. When she applied the same energy to uncovering my treasures, the same thing occurred. Barrier after barrier was found, and barrier after barrier broke to pieces before the power of our love and the ferocity of our will.

That has never stopped. Each level of depth we have achieved, we have had to disarm something. It is the job of the protective egoic mind to keep ourselves safe ... and full exposure *is not safe.*

One of the things we can do to make this process a little easier is be active on our end "being our own knight" in our own lives as much as we can. This is not just so things within us get uncovered, but so we get a little more used to having our guts exposed. That's honestly what it feels like; it feels like evisceration. And welcoming evisceration is not an easy thing to do. Dealing with evisceration as it happens is not easy. And being vulnerable, guts exposed, is not easy to handle.

So … get to practicing. Be willing.

I believe in my heart that this type of connection is important enough to be a life-sustaining motivation. The motivation to engage the opportunity to know the self and another through trailblazing effort … the motivation to allow someone to dig within us to find what may have eluded us about ourselves … these are life-fulfilling things. They are the most satisfying endeavors I have ever undertaken and followed through with.

The Cave we fear holds the treasure … where else would it be?

Things get tough when we're about to get deeper … where else would it get tough?

Things get uncomfortable when they need to be refined … where else would they get uncomfortable?

This is the reality of what we crave. It gets difficult *the second it's about to get real*. Why would it get difficult anywhere else?

Chapter 9:

Crappy Truths

There are crappy truths in life.

"Life is unfair."

"Good guys don't always win and cheaters don't always pay."

"Hard work is not always rewarded, and the best person for the job doesn't always get the job."

In life, these truths can stop us from evolving and working toward our goals if we do not take them in hand and incorporate their possibility into our reality. Basically? We can't EXPECT that we're not going to be dealing with some bullshit. It's gonna happen. It is going to happen to some of us more than others, and that's just the way it is.

Quick aside: I do not believe in Karma. I do not believe in justice (I like it, just don't believe it's a Universal law). I do not believe what goes around comes around. I do not believe that everything happens for a reason. If you do? Awesome! Just know that you don't need to believe in any of that to move forward and have a really good relationship with yourself, your partner, and the world.

The main crappy truth in relationships?

Pain is coming.

Pain Is Coming

There is no way around this. It's coming. Consider, the best-case scenario for any relationship is that we get to watch the person we really love get old, sick, and die. That's the best "result" we can hope for with the LEAST amount of pain.

The more life we experience, the more engaged we are, and the more generative we are in our families, the more we will have to suffer with and say goodbye to. This is reality. This is "the Process" of living in the world. It involves pain. And that's okay.

So, let's start with pain being okay. Let's start with it not being in our set of expectations that this life is going to be pain-free. Let's start there.

Next? Next, we have to know that some of the pain we experience and that our loved ones experience, is going to be because of us. Ugh. We are going to hurt each other. The closer and more intimate we are, the deeper and more powerfully we can hurt each other. Double ugh.

When we get married, one of our vows should be "I know I'm going to be the cause and reason for much of your pain, and I'm going to work my tail off to make it worth it for you." It may not seem romantic on wedding days, but exhausted to the bone and having money issues after the kids have stolen our energy and youth? It's important to realize what we promised, so we keep working to make our partner's pain worth it.

Every mistake we make with ourselves is going to affect the whole of the household. We have to know this. It's going to hurt, it's just also going to be worth it.

Why is this a big deal to me, in writing this book, that we accept that there is going to be pain, and do so in a conscious manner? Why does the obvious even have to be mentioned?

It has to be mentioned because mistakes can throw us so far off our game that we become *entirely different people* trying to manage ourselves in real time when they occur. If we were the ones that made the mistake, or the ones that caused the pain, then we have to deal with guilt and the want to put the blame elsewhere, which causes more damage. If it is our partner, we have to manage our anger so as not to hurt them. If it is our children, we have to be kind, patient parents. If it is life itself that jacks us up? Then we have to manage our internal fury and disappointment without targeting the rest of the family.

That's why it mandates attention and why I'm mentioning it.

Because basically, as Mike Tyson said: "Everyone has a plan … until they get hit."

Being the Bad Guy and Managing Guilt

Quite simply, this was the most difficult part for me, and it was also the most shocking. I did not even know how big of a deal it was. I can guarantee that in reading this book, for many, this will end up being the most important part.

We are fallible beings. We know this; it isn't news. But when we are really in love, the idea of hurting the person we love most, no matter what the reason, is an absolute fucking horrorshow. We do NOT want to be the person that hurts the one we love. It violates something within us that we may not even know about. I say this because I didn't know about it. So I know it's at least possible that others don't know either.

The first egoic reaction after making a mistake that hurts the one we love, is placing blame elsewhere. Most people do not get past this reaction.

What we need to do, regardless of whether it was intentional, carelessness, or total misunderstanding, is to stop … stay in the moment … and take our freaking medicine. Nothing hurts an injured person worse than being told BY THE ONE WHO HURT THEM that it's their fault they're hurt. That is something we simply can't do if we want to keep a healthy intimate relationship going. If it was unintentional, they'll figure it out later. But for now, just sit and LISTEN to the person you love and *feel the pain*.

Often, the pain we cause is tapping into pain that has been originally dealt to them by others, or *worsened* by others in the past. This is seductive for us, because it gives us a logical and foundationally supported way of *getting out of the discomfort*. But we can't. We have to endure it.

The second egoic reaction that can be damaging is to try to get the person out of the pain as fast as possible rather than allowing them process at their own speed. Why? Because we are empathizing with their pain (thus, feeling pain), feeling our own guilt, and having to process all of it at once.

Guess what? We can do that without rushing the other person. We can just manage our own business and process our own pain, frustration, and guilt. We can. It's not asking too much, because when we do this, it strengthens our core of integrity, as well as the relationship.

The third is more subtle and the most damaging. We want

to run so that we never hurt our loved one again. This is the spot where men and women run from relationships.

We are so resistant to hurting our partner, so unwilling to process our mistakes, so unprepared to be the bad guy for five minutes that we would actually rather just bolt from the whole thing.

We may be told that "everyone makes mistakes" and "no one is perfect," but we are not told "You are going to have to watch your mistakes hurt the people you care most about, and there isn't a damn thing you can do about it."

It is my personal belief that we hate this so much that we would rather make ridiculous mistakes and inflict a ton of pain to get broken up with ... so that we don't have to risk making HONEST mistakes while REALLY TRYING. I think this is a huge part of the cycle of low-self-worth/sabotage/inferiority-complex/acting-out that we see people play out over and over, but it's *nearly impossible to prove.*

So what do we do?

We eat crow and we learn to like it. We learn that being there for someone we've hurt without running or blaming gives them an opportunity to process the momentary pain and gain a deepened state of trust with us. Honestly, it's the same thing we would want to do with our kids.

Case in point ... when my youngest got off the bus and no one was home to let him in the house, and he freaked out? I REALLY wanted to blame the bus driver for being early because he was a stupid substitute! How was I supposed to know they were going to be early?! And honestly, I had everything timed perfectly! But my son was in distress, totally freaked. So was I going to worry about my anger at the bus driver … or tend to his needs in real time as I was needed?

"I'm sorry, it's my fault. I should have been here. It won't happen again."

That's it; then I sat there and let him get all his frustration out. Ten minutes later he said it wasn't my fault because the bus driver was driving crazy fast and scaring everyone. I didn't rush him so that I could feel better. I didn't even explain with an obvious excuse. *I honored his process and his emotional reality first.* By allowing myself to be the bad guy, I made sure nothing would be resisting the flow of communication between us.

Take a moment, now, and think about how many times you've tried to escape these moments. I'd suggest writing five down with five different people. Don't think of it as homework or busy work. Think of this as the part of this chapter that you are writing *to* yourself.

We all do it. We are so scared and uncomfortable feeling fault and guilt that we make everything so much worse by bailing on those we love when they need us most. I still have to stop myself from doing it, and I've been consciously aware of it for five years.

Just take a moment … this chapter is called "Crappy Truths" for a reason. Do some writing.

There is a reason we have to acknowledge these truths. We have to acknowledge these truths because of the Hypothetical Imperative.

The Hypothetical Imperative (source: Immanuel Kant) is an "if-then" statement. If we want ____, we must _____. This goes back to the assumptions I made chapters ago. I assume, if you're reading this, that you want deep intimacy and deep satisfaction from your relationship. If you do want that, there are going to be some truly crappy moments that you are going to have to hit head on and power through like a champ.

Why? Because that is what leads to deep intimacy and deep satisfaction. You simply can't have it without going through some messy, uncomfortable, painful moments. You can't. Marilyn Monroe's quote caught my eye when I was young, and I dismissed it as "stuff hot chicks say to not be accountable for themselves," because I simply had no real experience dealing with human beings other than my parents. It may be one of the simplest and most direct expressions of feminine (and masculine) relationship reality that there is.

Translating Marilyn

"If you can't handle me at my worst, you don't deserve me at my best."

This seems kind of combative and aggressive upon first look, but it's not. It's just a description of the hypothetical imperative for intimacy from the first-person perspective.

What she is actually saying, is "If you cannot manage my worst moments without freaking out, I'm not going to feel safe around you. If I do not feel safe around you, I will not be able to be myself around you. If I am not able to be myself around you, neither of us is going to have any fun."

That needs to be plastered everywhere, because it's only obvious AFTER it's understood. How much fun do we have with people we don't feel safe with? How much fun do we have when we're uncomfortable? How do we possibly think that anyone else is going to be fun, or have fun with us, when they don't feel safe? How are they going to feel safe, if WE DO NOT PROVIDE SAFETY?

This is almost more like math than psychology. Both men and women need to feel safe to have fun. Both men and women need to feel safe to sustain a sexual relationship with each other (not "have sex," but sustain a sexual relationship over years). Both men and women need to feel safe to be able to relax.

Can we always provide safety? No. Sometimes we aren't enough. Hell, sometimes enough doesn't exist. But that's not our business. Our business is to give it every single ounce of effort we have ... and then see what happens.

This set up is overwhelming when we first look at it, and overwhelming the first few times we engage it. But there is no way to get deep intimacy and satisfaction without it. Creating safety is the job of both parties in the relationship, and that means that we "parent when needed, not when convenient."

That means being the bad guy when it comes up. It means soaking up emotional overflow when it happens. It means being patient when we are fed up. It means staying present when we are exhausted. It means holding reactivity when we are fired up. It means not blaming the Divine Partner for the way that they process their world.

That's the work. The only way "around" the work ... is OUT of the relationship. Many accidentally choose that because they don't know any better. They don't know that you can't skip out on someone else's processes without ABANDONING THEM.

This is the work, this is the job. If we don't do the job (presence), we don't get the pay (intimacy).

Do the job, or be willing to walk away … the FIT

Please. Don't. Waste. Precious. Time.

I have a huge reaction to half measures and stringing people along. I have a huge reaction to wasting someone's time when someone who could truly want to be with them is possibly waiting for an opportunity. For me, that's like incarcerating an innocent.

We might just think this is when leeching off a strong person, so that it doesn't apply to us. But it's not. It's also *when we are putting up with or enabling a person we believe to be weak*. We may even feel like we're doing them a favor. But we're keeping them from someone who truly wants them.

Whatever someone's processes are, that's our job to honor. IT IS OUR JOB TO HONOR OUR PARTNER'S PROCESSES. If we don't want to do that, that's fine. We just have to leave. No excuses, no blaming bullshit, no reasoning … *just leave*.

We believe someone's processes are abusive? Awesome. Leave.

We are burdened and not looking forward to how they process emotion? Awesome. Leave.

We are unsatisfied with their mood swings? Leave.

What we don't do? We don't pretend like we're putting up with them to make ourselves feel better at the expense of them finding someone they FIT with. Because honestly, it's not them, and it's not you. It's the FIT. And if the fit is wrong, staying with them keeps you BOTH from finding the right fit, and that is honestly the biggest waste of life there is.

Now, have no doubt, we can learn to love and enjoy *just about everything* under the Sun. If we don't? It's because …

1) We can't

Or

2) We're not willing.

In the first case, we need to move on because the fit isn't right. There are plenty of relationships where both people are trying 150% and it's just not going to work. Again, this chapter is on Crappy Truths. Sometimes there's no good fit, and that's okay.

In the second case, we need to move on because we are not ready to do what it takes to be in a relationship. Sometimes we're not ready to do what's needed; that's okay too. It's okay.

What's not okay is pretending that it's working or pretending that we're ready. There's evidence. We know deep down, and it takes effort to obfuscate that truth. We all will waste some time doing this, because we believe ourselves to be a failure if we can't make something work. We may also waste time because we don't know what "not working" is ... because we've never seen "working" in our lives. But ... we know when we look at the evidence. We're unsatisfied. They're unsatisfied. No one is having fun anymore. We get upset when they're around. We get excited about being around other people and dread being with our partners.

If we don't want the job, the evidence is there. That means it's time to step aside and let *someone who wants the job* have a crack at it.

People are really difficult to get along with. Relationships are really hard. I don't blame anyone for bailing. I DO blame people for hanging on when there is nothing but soul-destroying safety to keep them together.

Part of living with integrity is "looking" with integrity. That "looking" leads to "knowing and wisdom." That leads to action.

We're not helping someone by staying with them when it's not working. Regardless of what they say they want. We're robbing them of the most precious gift anyone has ... opportunity.

Who do we want to be? This is really the question of this chapter (and of the book, honestly).

There are some really difficult duties to take on when seeking commune with another human being. Do we want to be the kind of person who gets excited by the challenge and frustration? Or do we want to be the kind of person who bails and then looks for justification in blaming the other?

In the end, most of this book is saying that "desire + integrity = joyful union," while showing the aspects of our ego's *natural inclination to seek to rob us* of that desire and integrity so that we cannot risk the changes that come with union. The Crappy Truths are an area where the ego can grasp evidence and hold on tight, giving it the authority of fear over our decision-making, and then rob us of our opportunities. But when we know its tricks, and how it operates, it gets very difficult to just allow it to enslave us at the expense of our souls.

Chapter 10:

Part 1 ... Know Your Tragedy.
Rewriting in real time.

Every relationship comes with many possible scripts. Each person brings their own story in and the setting of the relationship also provides a lot of content. In the old dramatic world (Greece) there were only Comedy and Tragedy, and they were defined in a different manner than they are commonly known today.

Comedy was not just "containing humor" ... but had to end in resolution of differences and very specifically ***a marriage***. Tragedy was not just "bad things befall the characters" but more specifically a "fatal flaw" would lead the main character to his death through a series of poor *impulsive* decisions. In the definitions of old-school tragedy, "impulsive" was not really the word they tossed around as being vital to the issues that would lead to the main character's tragic end. They were bigger on hubris. However, when I watch them, it is generally emotionally motivated errors in judgment that cause the demise in a tragedy.

When we enter a relationship of any kind, we always see the comedy. We see the characters getting married after going through some hardships possibly and everyone coming together through their union to create a larger family. If we aren't seeing that at the beginning of a relationship, we generally don't get in one.

The truth, though, is that *basically every relationship we will ever be in is a Tragedy*. And only by knowing ourselves truly and deeply can we understand and influence **what kind of Tragedies we are co-creating**.

Know the script.

We all have a set of scripts. When we get into a relationship we all have to pair that script with someone else's script and hope for a Comedy. Unfortunately, we're a messy species these days, and we have a ton of wounds. Even if we aren't resistant to healing (which *most* are, as it demands engaging the wounds), the number of wounds we have make Tragedies the expected form of drama between any two people. This is just how it is now. We're unskilled at *rewriting* in real time.

The question is, do we know our **Tragic Script**? Do we know the script of our lovers? Do we know how they fit together to potentially destroy everything we care about? Are we conscious of our abilities to rewrite in real time if necessary?

If we know these things, then we can align ourselves as a team, a union "in opposition to" how that Tragic Script wants to play out. When we can steer and influence our lives away from those scripted moments, we have taken on an empowered role in our **Relationship Life**. That makes us a good partner to hook up with and gives us confidence as we move through life. It does NOT mean we aren't going to have crappy breakups and make mistakes. It just means that we aren't being completely driven by the things that have happened to us before into *predictable* mistakes. Predictable, preventable, and REPETITIVE mistakes. Basically, it gives our relationship an opportunity for authenticity, maybe even a shot at being a Comedy.

In our Relationship Life, the identity we have as a partner that evolves with us over time, we have carried with us the entire mess of our history. Yes, the Mess. Capital M-E-S-S. This includes our relationship history and tendencies to repeat and project, as well as the basic Prime Issues men and women have already ground into them from their Biological Imperative. All of those aspects push the script.

The job we have in regard to our Relationship Life's characteristics hinges on our knowledge of this script. If we know this script … we can protect ourselves and those we love from the nasty things our script wants to push us into doing. But we have to know it. We have to accept the fact that it exists and know what behaviors we are being "pushed" into.

As an alcoholic, I know really well that my escapism will draw me away from my Divine Other and toward a bottle, and that I will be moved to hold her responsible for these actions (yes, hold her responsible for MY actions) in order to justify them. I will get anxious, blame her for the anxiety, and start drinking. That's just something we addicts do. We're awesome at it.

That's just ONE example of my script. In this case, it is one part addict (booze) one part Prime Issue (escape). But it's still scripted. And it hurts those I love.

If I let the script dominate my behavior patterns, I will resent her, she will become more critical of my behaviors, and I will bail. That's one version of how the full script could play out. In general, that would mesh well with any woman's script of being used, unappreciated, and abandoned, so the confluence would not be difficult to achieve. I came into my relationship with my dear love KNOWING that was what would happen *if I wasn't actively rewriting in real time*. I knew it. And in knowing it, I stopped it from happening.

In this culture, we rarely talk about how we're going to fail. I have suggested conversations to couples I've mentored about "having a plan for how you want to break up," and exactly ZERO of them have thought it was a good idea. I love that. I love the deep and primal resistance to looking at the possibility of breaking up.

In the same way, I see people often very resistant to looking at how they are most likely to mess up a relationship given their history and personal tendencies. What I don't see is "why."

Hand it over.

The scripts that we carry are often filled with humiliating garbage. That's a bummer for the ego. But the goal is to get them out and try to hand them to our partner. Yes, our PARTNER. We do this so they can help us not repeat our mistakes. It's like a cheat sheet on our own bullshit. Giving our partner the direct line to our ego's crap *so that we can team up against it* (doesn't that sound amazing?). And honestly, the conversations get pretty cool when BOTH scripts get pulled out and analyzed.

"This is how I like to sabotage myself!"

"Oh yeah? I do that too!"

"This is how I will attack you if I get scared, and you may

be able to tell beforehand because I do this ____ (insert behavior here)."

"Okay, cool! My impulse control is really bad in all of these areas, and then I selectively forget about what happened and will accuse you of possible insanity when you remember things differently than I did. That's one of my favorites."

"NICE, that's a GOOD one ... I'll totally be on the lookout for that! One of my things is to also live in a kind of fantasy land where things are easier and better in other relationships, or that they could be if I was with other people, and I won't tell you about it because I have a hard time realizing when it's happening!"

"Oh that's going to work awesome with my assumption that I'm going to be left for another person! We have to keep a really close eye on that one--whew!"

Yeah. These are conversations that NEED to be had.

One of the big fears *we tell ourselves we have* is that the people we hand our fears to will use them against us, or that we will be seen as weak. That's not our fear. Our ACTUAL fear is that the person *will call us on our bullshit*. That they will call us out for running our Tragic Script. Believe me, it's infuriating when my mate calls me out on the first couple steps of a panic attack I'm trying to indulge in the hopes of escaping whatever is making me uncomfortable.

You may tell yourself that you're frightened that they will think you're weak (as if being powerfully vulnerable could ever be seen as weak), but in actuality someone being able to catch us in the middle of our sabotaging and call us out is a real danger to the *plight of the ego*. So, the ego lies and tells us the other may not like us if they know our weaknesses.

Why? Because we're addicted to the illusion of control. We want to let our script play out and pretend we couldn't do anything about it. It's the easiest thing, and it is risk-free, from an accountability standpoint. It allows our heart to stay closed and keeps us from the risk of growth and change.

So what's your script? I'm asking. I have been the martyr, the aloof father figure, the betrayed, and the abused (for a few). That's all before I was twenty-four. I had all these ways to keep myself safely capable of sabotage. I even used some roles to create other roles. Like the poor players from Chapter 4 wandering around in the dark trying to figure out how to hug without getting hurt? I actually became an alcoholic during one of my later incarnations of the "martyr."

What's yours? Think about it. Like, right now, put the book down, and go write out the titles you'd give yourself as you aided in ending the relationships you've been in ... the roles you've played while helping steer the ship into the cliffs. You can see them ... you aren't blind to who you've been. Now empower yourself by being conscious of that script going forward. Own it.

This is how we start the Rewriting process of our Relationship Life.

Rewriting the script is based on the idea that we can only make changes when the script is challenged, either by us or by our partner, while the activation is occurring. This makes rewriting *difficult*, while it's *not exactly complicated*.

It is based on the idea that simply "trying something different" in a situation where we may be driven to behave in a predictable or repetitive way can not only help in the moment, but undermine the dominance of the scripts that we run. It's also kinda fun, if I haven't mentioned that.

Rewriting: How We Keep From Making the Same Mistakes

One of the issues with rewriting is that *since it is new* to us as we are doing it, *it is naturally uncomfortable*. Discomfort stops us from doing a lot of healthy things, especially when it comes to making healthy changes.

It is natural for us to keep behaving the same way in relationships because it is in line with our egoic need for stasis, but it generally brings about the same reality, which is likely what ENDED the last relationship. In fact, going into each NEW relationship, we should be looking at what aspects we want to do "totally differently."

If we do not act differently than we did in our last relationship, *how can we expect a different result*?

In this way, "Knowing our Tragedy" can lead directly to the habit of rewriting. Recognizing patterns within ourselves can lead to the implantation of **Self-Created Triggers**. Self-Created Triggers are tools used to keep us from repeating behaviors that do not lead to healthy consequences.

The best way to describe these is by thinking of behaviors within a relationship as a minefield (it's probably not the first time you've felt like you were in a minefield in a relationship, right?) … but instead of worrying about where we're stepping now, we have to PLACE mines over our old patterns so that we avoid them in the NEW relationship.

"Hmmm, I was avoidant here when I felt nervous about discussing ____, and that led to resentment and aggression before. So what I'm going to do is place a little land mine on my old footprints."

One of the difficulties here (and also the fun, if we can get ourselves into the perspective) is that we don't have another set of footsteps to follow through the field. There is uncertainty, and that can be paralyzing. But ... IT'S LESS PARALYZING IF WE KNOW IT'S COMING. Even less paralyzing than that if we understand that we are consciously choosing it, and that it is for relationship health reasons.

Then we can move forward ... and THAT is what rewriting is all about. That is how we change the script ... we toss the old story and engage our willingness to try something different.

I know my Tragedy. I know it because I looked at it over and over. That recognition and awareness naturally led to me seeking new paths of behavior. And since seeking the new is also a courageous act, doing so made me stronger and more capable as a partner.

The main idea behind Knowing our Tragedy is that we're trying not to repeat it. When we see a new relationship, we don't want to think "I am really looking forward to resenting them in a year or so."

We want to be able to move forward with some confidence. That takes focus, conscious effort, and practice. And all of those take EXPERIENCE. There's no way around that.

So knowing what we know now, how do we want to engage as we move into intimacy with another person? We want to try to make it a little better than the last time we tried, and we want to make the Tragedies conscious. We want to do this so that we can work on them together in a state of mutual respect.

Managing the Tragedies ... okay, so now, can we like, not do that?

"Now that we know ourselves, and have told each other about what our tendencies are, can't we like, help each other not repeat the same mistakes?"

I think so. Of course, there has to be mutual respect, and no resentment built up already, but it's absolutely doable if we commit to making it a part of our conscious presence. It seems easy when we read it, but it's a tough task when it comes up.

It's something "we don't want to bother" our new relationship with. That's like not bothering the driver to tell him we're almost out of gas on a road trip in the desert. *It saves us from a tiny discomfort now and ensures devastation later.*

One of the things that gets in the way of this is that it is seen as unsexy rather than sexy. This is because we have not yet habituated respectful connection through vulnerability as sexy in our culture.

I remember my brother telling me about condoms when I was fifteen. He said "Hey, you're not going to want to slow down and take three minutes, and she may not want to either, but it's really disrespectful and juvenile to not protect yourself and the person you're with. Just take a second and try to make it fun rather than this awful chore, and then you'll both be safer and you can relax."

That's the same thing. At the beginning of new relationships, in the honeymoon period … we don't want to talk about this kind of stuff, makes us feel "human," rather than like "giant magical unicorns" (yes, that's what I feel like), and is kind of a buzzkill. But it can save the relationship. And honestly, what is sexier than that?

So talk about it. Say, "Hey, this is my behavior pattern, and that's yours. So now we can reality check each other if we start noticing things. I'll be kind about it and not harp or nag or step on your toes, if you will show me the same courtesy."

If you get used to doing it young, it will save you TONS of frustration. It will also make you strong. It IS taking OWNERSHIP of our shit. It's empowering, as every step into deeper self-accountability is.

Chapter 10:

Part 2: Unfuckable
(How to Destroy Your Sex Life)

It's easy to kill attraction. Really easy.

Attraction is generated by the harmonic connection of two bodies. It is not a decision we can make or a feeling we can control. There is nothing about a relationship's chemistry that can be controlled by will alone.

This can be horrifically frustrating, because sometimes the chemistry just vanishes for no apparent reason. Generally, though, there's a good reason to explain why it disappeared. This is what I am going to focus on during this chapter.

STOP BEING A SHITTY ROOMMATE.

Don't litter … and pull your weight. This is basic roommate advice.

Intimacy is awesome. Sharing space is awesome. But have no doubts that when sharing space, even before moving in together, we have to show the people we share space with a ton of respect *IF we want to remain attractive to them*. This is not about chores and housework … it is about respect.

Respect for the space, comfort, and sensibilities of the person we are with. We're going to want to respect their pet peeves, too. This basic willingness to compromise, while obvious in roommate situations, seems to get lost often in relationships. I have no idea where this sense of entitlement comes from, but it doesn't translate into lasting sexual connection.

If we're shitty roommates? We're gonna make ourselves unfuckable.

Littering and not pulling our weight are tangible issues. They are easily discussed if we are the remotest bit willing to self-examine and adjust. Littering is not just "being messy" with clothes and cookware, it is being **undisciplined about our effect on our shared environment**. Sometimes this is physical, sometimes it is emotional, sometimes financial.

When someone has to clean up urine in the bathroom because of poor aim?

When checks bounce in shared accounts because someone didn't bother to check before spending?

When someone gets into a fit of anger and busts a hole in the wall or breaks dishes?

When someone gets too drunk and gets out of hand in a social setting?

When someone is in a situation that affects their mood, but while they will complain about it (not vent, note the choice of words) they won't do anything to change it?

When someone is super critical of the other and seeks every opportunity to correct and micro-manage because they are undisciplined with their need to control?

When someone cannot control what words they use during an argument or processing and they end up severely injuring the other?

When someone is habitually blaming the other for anything that happens?

When someone can't stop playing video games or get off their phone to connect?

When someone leaves messes for the other to take care of?

When one person needs to process and the other refuses because it makes them uncomfortable?

When one person does much more work than the other?

Yeah … NONE OF THAT IS SEXY. If we can't pull our weight and keep our house-hygiene decently managed, at some point the person we are with is going to look at us with one of the following …

1) Resentment

2) Embarrassment

Neither of those feelings makes it possible to sustain attraction.

This isn't something that we need to argue about amongst each other, because everyone is different. Standards of cleanliness, pet peeves, emotional comfort, and personal hygiene all vary from person to person. This isn't about what someone or "people in general" SHOULD want. It is about what the person we have hitched our lives to *DOES want from us*.

I have an ex who needed the cupboards closed. I dismissed her request, reasoning that it made no sense. And it doesn't make sense. But the actual reason I didn't do it *is because I was lazy, and not interested in changing my behavior* to make her more comfortable.

We don't want to be that person anymore, do we?

We don't want to argue and quibble on behalf of our laziness to get out of providing comfort, do we? Is that really us? Wouldn't we rather just take the opportunity to step into a larger role of responsibility in regard to meeting the needs of the person we love?

Case in point: doing dishes. When I'm done doing dishes, I have an empty sink and a clear countertop. For my mate, this is NOT clean … why? Because it's still wet. My first reaction was "Well, the water is clean, so your rule is silly, I'm not going to accommodate that." But that is not what I want. I WANT to accommodate her. So I take a sec, and I think: *Why might she have a different idea of clean … hmmm … maybe it's from ten years in the Navy?*

Yes. It was that. Her standards of clean are different from mine, and regardless of what I think about them, they exist. So I have the choice … I can clean to her standards, or I can whine and resist because I don't want to take *an extra thirty seconds* to finish the job.

The guy that I am now wipes the wetness off so that when she sees the sink, her mind doesn't get caught on the fact that the job isn't done. The guy I am now would have closed the cupboards, too.

There are so many ways we can pull our weight and not litter, so many ways we can slowly make our partner's lives easier in ways that they wouldn't even think to ask. The idea is not that we HAVE to stress about these things, but that if we commit to looking for them we can really enjoy finding them when they pop into our consciousness.

There are so many things in life that make everything we do more difficult. Why not commit to being a source of "making life easier" for those we are with?

The thing is, when we're in a relationship, we assume that our sexual needs are going to be met by the other person *based on the fact that we are in a relationship, rather than by how we are behaving in that relationship.*

We aren't owed JACK.

We assume somehow that we are owed something when in a relationship. We aren't.

We think because we share a bed with someone, or finances, that we are guaranteed sexual access? Bullshit. There is probably a large school of thought thinking that this is mainly males expecting it of females ... but from what I've seen, it's about even.

In both cases, we forget that we are not entering into sexual activity with a marriage license, a written contract, a lawyer, or even a person's mind. We are dealing with body parts and subconscious psychology. We deal with blood flow, wetness, relaxation, and confidence. We don't **decide** to be turned on ... we either are or we aren't. Sexual relationships are based on mutual respect and safety, so that a pure version of "play" can be achieved.

If a man lets his woman down consistently, why would she

feel safe? If she doesn't feel safe, how can she get aroused? If she doesn't respect him and believe in who he is … how can her body respond to his advances?

If a woman is overly critical or doesn't do her part, how can a man feel excited? If she has alienated him, how can she expect his body to respond?

It's not about what we can talk our partners into, it's about what our behavior inspires from their body. Sexual connectedness is **continued inspiration** … not a contract. If we are not inspiring or we find it impossible to be inspired by our partner … that's the end of it. There is no arguing that will change it. That is what I am really trying to teach … so that it doesn't keep happening to everyone.

It's not about what we expect or can reason should be the case, it's about *inspiring another person's body to respond positively to us*. That's it. We are owed nothing.

I want to reiterate what I said at the beginning of the chapter. This is NOT about what things should be like or how people should behave. This is just a warning. The warning is simple …

If we do not pull our weight and inspire respect from our partner and they lose interest in us? There is not a damn thing we can do about it. There are no arguments that can be had and won, no reasoned line of thinking that can activate desire. I am really hoping to keep everyone engaged in the inspirational aspects that the initial attraction was founded on, so that we don't have the absolute mess that is created when respect is lost and cannot be found.

There are many people in the world who do not want this to be the truth. They want a world where sexual desire is ensured and controlled. They want a world where they do not have to be account-able for the effect their behavior has on their own desirability. It's okay for them to want that. They just can't have it, because it doesn't exist. And we may not be able to convince them, we may just have to leave. That's okay, too.

There is a lot we can do to make sure it doesn't come to this, and that's where our energy should be going. That's where mine is going as I write this chapter. After this? I'll be cleaning the kitchen and mak-ing the coffee for tomorrow morning.

Chapter 11:

The Hangover Proposal for Relationships ...

In *Coffee for Consciousness 101* I dedicated an entire chapter to the Hangover Proposal, because I feel it to be the best description for why people make self-sabotaging decisions. We prefer the illusion of control that comes with making a bad decision over the anxiety of risking ourselves to make a good one.

I'll just copy and paste that description here straight from the other book.

The Therapist's Query

So ... a therapist put out an open question one night in frustration: "Why does someone come to therapy, pay me money, listen to my advice, and then completely ignore it in the face of all evidence over a long period of time?!"

This is a good question, and the answer is not obvious until you hear it. Afterwards, it is forever super obvious. We have been distracted by individual psychoanalysis and missed a commonality that has far-reaching effects. Everyone ignores advice and everyone finds a way to not do what's best for them. The reason however, is not specific to the person.

DOING WHAT'S BEST IS NOT A SURE THING. THERE IS NO GUARANTEE IT WILL WORK.

SABOTAGING OUR LIVES WORKS EVERY TIME.

The second behavior is simply more satisfying.

Happiness is not guaranteed, no matter what. You can do your absolute best, study and practice and meditate and focus all your positive energy on loving the world and healthy relating ... and get the short end of the stick.

THAT IS HORRIBLE! The injustice of it is simply too much to take. I still can't handle it all that well.

So, what do we do with that subconscious knowledge? What do we do knowing that we can't have the power to *ensure* the *happiness* and *safety* we crave?

We decide that we'd rather prove to ourselves that we're *powerful* by actively sabotaging our lives, making bad decisions (as bad decisions *almost always* lead to negative consequences). We choose to be powerful instead of taking a chance at being happy. We can always cause ourselves pain. So when we feel helpless and scared, *we load the gun and shoot our own feet*.

Homer Simpson to Lisa on *The Simpsons*: "Aww, Lisa, look here now, you tried your best, and you failed miserably. The lesson is ... never try."

That's literally what we do. We choose the risk-free option.

We do make ourselves feel better by asking for help, venting, and going to therapy. It's the same as having a gym membership and never going. It makes us feel good to use it as defense if people question our commitment to health and well-being (and you better have a defense ... because you can't righteously complain without one ... oops).

So when we look at someone who won't take advice and we are resentful toward them for sabotaging their lives, it's important to know why they are doing it. The need for power and control looms large in our frightened adult conscious-ness. It will keep us from ever taking the chances our soul came here to take.

This is why we can ignore good advice and sabotage our lives. It is a very seductive power we wield, and I fully under-stand that we may not want to give it up. But now we know why we bail on good advice, and hopefully, knowing "why" will influence every conversation we have from now on (in-ternal and external conversations).

When someone says "it's too hard," they don't mean it's actually too difficult. They mean there's no assurance it will make them happy, so it's not worth how hard it is.

When we look at the people in our lives through this perspective, the mistakes everyone make and the advice they ignore becomes less of a mystery and more of a simple behavior pattern. This perspective has helped me refine my environment a lot. When someone is not ready to help themselves and we don't know why, it is difficult to make a judgment call on whether to keep helping them or not. But when we know why they are not helping themselves, we can take ac-tion more easily, and we should.

It is frustrating when someone screams for food, and then tosses into the garbage the three-course meal we've set in front of them. We don't have to be frustrated, though. We can just know that they are afraid of the risk, and afraid of giving up certainty. I want to use another analogy to highlight the issue, and in this analogy I will use myself as the example of the person ignoring advice.

The Hangover Proposal

For many years in my twenties I was a drunk. Not just a year or two … many. During this time, I discovered many things about myself. I became well acquainted with my personal psychology, not just as an addict (which is really informative on its own), but as a person with a mixture of needs and compulsions that expressed themselves in many ways. Drinking was always an answer to a problem, but I was very focused on what all of these "problems" were. And, because I had no intention of "not drinking" anytime soon, the pressure was off for me to bullshit myself, and I was afforded the ability to watch the natural expression of my psychology.

Every day I had a choice: "Stop drinking if you want to feel better." This is a true statement I considered every day. True as the world turning. But I didn't stop. I didn't stop drinking for so many reasons that the cumulative number of reasons I didn't stop became a reason to drink. It was obvious that I should stop drinking if I wanted to feel better, but there was a catch. While I felt bad when I was drinking, it didn't mean that if I stopped drinking that I would feel good.

So, let's take a look at detox. It's SOOOO fun. You feel awful for two or three days, and then you feel better. It's really great to feel better. Every day you wake up early, can participate in life, can complete basic tasks, etc. As you are going about being sober, you are faced with a question every day. "I am starting to feel bad, and I don't like it. If I drink, I'll feel better." This is another true statement. I'll feel better for a short time in trade for how I will feel the next morning. I'll be useless and unhappy most of the next day, in fact, and I know it.

Let me say right now, this is me after drinking for 5-6 years straight. That is a ton of liquor, all day. Many people can drink and be fine the next day. So when I say "I'll be useless tomorrow if I drink," that's just me.

So, knowing I would literally be "taking myself out" for the entire next day if I drank, I resisted temptation and worked through it. I stayed sober so that I could feel better the next day. Yay, me! But then, after resisting the urge to remove myself from an issue, the unthinkable happened. I woke up in a bad mood and had no energy. WAIT, THAT WASN'T THE DEAL I MADE!!!!!

I made the deal that I wasn't going to drink so that I would feel good the next day. This was just crazy and infuriating. I didn't feel good and I didn't even do anything wrong! Rude!

I felt *betrayed*. The next time I was faced with that decision, the nature of my options was different. I had what most see as a choice between feeling good and feeling bad, but it was actually the choice between "maybe feeling good," and "definitely feeling bad." This choice was very different. I know what a hangover is, *and I can choose it*. I CANNOT choose to feel good with certainty. It is not an option that is *guaranteed*.

In relationships, though, the reason is more complex. The sabotage-for-control is still in effect, but the culprit and accountable party is obscured by the presence of a "Blame Token." This person may be sick, abusive, addicted, unfaithful, mentally unstable, or any other description that puts their counterpart in the relationship "out of blame's way."

If we are with an addict or abuser (I find these to be the two most common, but there are others), while we may get a ton of flak for not leaving the relationship from friends and family, we will NEVER be seen *as the reason that the relationship isn't working*. When we are with someone who is incapable of giving even ten percent to a relationship, no one is going to check to see how much we are giving.

I know this from experience.

When I was with one of my most traumatic relationships with a Borderline Personality- disordered addict … while many would ask me why I was still with her, no one was challenging what I was bringing to the relationship. *That made me feel safe*. I didn't have to worry about holding up my end of the relationship, because when it went down (and it did) *it was going to be her fault no matter what*.

Mind you, I was a kid at the time, and I learned after a while what a cop-out it was for me to be the boyfriend I was with her. She deserved more than a warm body leeching martyrdom from her desperate state; she needed help. Help that I could not and did not provide.

So … why the Blame Token?

I get that hooking up with someone who is a really bad partner *sounds* like a bad idea, and becomes almost unbelievable (especially when we are self-examining) as a realistic option when thought of *logically through cultural norms*. Let me just stop you there. It's actually a really great option for most, and even logical.

This is what we get when you take a Blame Token as our partner.

1) Physical togetherness, someone to sleep next to (this is actually huge).

2) Someone to cause problems that distract us from the pressure of creating a life on our own.

3) Something to complain to our friends about.

4) A target for "reduced guilt" Anger Transference, as they either deserve it or won't remember it.

5) Someone to blame all our bullshit on. "If only I weren't constantly being held back by ____!"

6) A tether ... a ball and chain to keep us from being with someone who would challenge us.

7) Someone who will never see our deep weaknesses and fears because they are not present enough.

8) Someone we don't have to be faithful to or have integrity around.

9) Someone to blame it on when the ship goes down.

10) The ability to receive pity attention and pity support.

That's actually *a lot of perks*. We don't have to be a crazy narcissist or martyr or self-loathing fool to see that list and decide it may not be a bad idea. We just have to be two things ...

1) Scared

2) Ignorant of why we're doing it (so we don't have to be accountable to ourselves)

This isn't crazy. It makes perfect sense. But ... it's not healthy. Not for anyone. It hurts those involved and sets a really bad example for how relationships should be. This is the bond of betrayal, where both are instrumental in undermining growth for the sake of familiarity.

This is why I'm describing it. We can't really be ignorant about it after reading it. We may still do it, of course, but at some point, we're going to realize it.

Now, this does not mean that some relationships that others have that look like this to us, ARE this way. Some people value different things. Some people are happy in really interesting scenarios. The red flag we want to look for when trying to assess relationships that may fit into this category (which we should just be doing *with ourselves*, or people who are consistently complaining to us and draining our energy) is what values are placed over growth.

Is loyalty being placed above desire and growth? Is guilt being placed above it? Is comfort being placed above it? Money? The kids (this is the worst one, and the most often used)?

Those are the red flags.

We are coming into an age of *facing dissonance*. We are coming into an age of having the time and safety to truly know ourselves and to honor our love and desire. No one has had this before, so it's not supposed to be easy. It's supposed to scare us to death. Having a Blame Token works to keep some of us from facing things we do not want to, but that is not going to move society forward. It isn't going to help us open our collective heart, and that is what we need.

Chapter 12

The Beauty of Being Trapped

Every relationship involves a job. Every relationship has a way it fits or doesn't fit. Every relationship ... except a relationship among multiple people working together. Going into this chapter is a tad nerve-racking for me because I know it's a touchy subject and I simply do not want to be misunderstood. So, I'm going to say a few things right at the outset.

I am NOT saying what anyone should or should not do. I may suggest that certain things are possible in one setting and impossible in another. Some things are possible in monogamy that are not in polyamory and vice versa. Whether you want those are based on YOUR values and desires, and regardless of what you take my meanings to be in this chapter, I will tell you now in advance that I LOVE both styles and know them both from many angles. I want every person to HONOR their DESIRES ... that's my entire position on the subject of "which one is better."

When I say "polyamory," I am using it LOOSELY. There are many different types and differing levels of seriousness. Some involve contracts and others are just open relationships. I am going to use "polyamory" as the word denoting anything along those lines in order to save time. If you are curious about different types of these practices, I invite you to look the subject up online.

What I am doing in this chapter, mainly, is using polyamory as a foil to show certain aspects of relationships that *show up only when comparing* these relationship styles.

The main difference between polyamory and monogamy has to do with whether or not we're trapped (no joke, huh?). The question we need to ask ourselves is *whether or not we want the intimacy that comes from being trapped with someone.*

The Beauty of Being Trapped

I rarely talk about being in a twin flame relationship, because most self-described Twin Flames have a different perspective on life than I do.

Very simply, if my Claudia were sentenced to prison, I would choose to be locked in a cell with her for however many years she was sentenced, rather than being free. Even if it was for the rest of my life. Period. Why? Because our relationship is so deep (bottomless) that there is more freedom with her in a tiny cell than there is in the rest of the world. She's my home, and there is nothing else that comes close.

I know, I'm a romantic. But ... I'm also not bullshitting. Not one bit.

Our desire to be with one another traps us. I am trapped with her, and *I want to be trapped.* What does that mean?

It means that no one saves me but her, and no one saves her but me. When anything goes wrong we have each other to go to, no one else.

That's the way I want it. I want the person I am with to be the one I trust with everything. That means that every mistake I make is in her lap. It means that I HAVE to be accountable for all of my behavior, because I don't have anywhere else to go. I think putting all of my eggs in one basket is the greatest compliment I could give to any person, and I have no interest in being with anyone whom I don't love and respect that much.

Being trapped with her means I can't run from my failures. *Being trapped with her means I can't hurt myself without hurting her and having to be accountable for that AND whatever guilt comes with it.* Being trapped with her means that whatever she brings into the relationship is now MINE, and anything I bring in is now HERS.

Why would anyone want that? Why would anyone want to be trapped?

Because when you believe that someone is the greatest thing ever built on the face of the Earth and your heart and mind become naturally and totally devoted to their existence ... wanting all of that crazy stuff is the highest HONOR you can imagine.

When they choose to be trapped WITH you ... heaven opens and you both get to go inside for as long as you can keep it together. But that is a conscious CHOICE for us. A choice based on honoring the desire flowing through our veins.

That is Healthy Monogamy ... monogamy based on desire, rather than monogamy based on control and insecurity. Monogamy based on desire is based on wanting the best for our partners. This means that if what is best for our partners includes something non-monogamous, while we may be hurt as hell, we *wouldn't ever stop them from moving on or out* if that's what they needed to be happy. We just know going in that we have more to offer than anyone else on the planet for the person we love and who loves us.

This is the beauty and power of being trapped. I want to be the person she comes to, forever, because I have more to offer her than the rest of the world combined. When we see that with each other, and our life together bears that out, we feel totally fulfilled.

But that is NOT what everyone wants, and it is not what is fulfilling *for everyone*.

Monogamy based on control and insecurity is what I call "Mate Hoarding." This means that while we may not want to let the person we're with fully grow or be there for them completely, we are certainly not going to let them go get satisfied elsewhere, because it makes us look bad. That is monogamy based on control and need. There is quite a lot of that. So … since we can't fully access the riches of the person we're with (because we don't want to try or because we're a bad fit), we're going to make sure no one else can either.

Being in an unfulfilling relationship is the waste of the glorious gift of life we have all been given, and not yielding to our desires to expand our hearts when asked is like turning on a Ferrari and leaving it running in a garage forever. Obviously, I am not a fan.

I like being trapped. Polyamory is not my thing. I know truly that polyamory not only serves a purpose for people who abhor being tied down or trapped with anyone, but it serves a greater role of freeing us from the garbage expectations that we may have inherited from a *sexually repressed and unsatisfied culture* while we were growing up. It gives us something that we may not learn anywhere else, and that is how to HONOR the desires of someone we love.

The Loosening of the Ego

The nature of the Egoic Mind is pretty consistent. It wants ownership and control. It wants to be safe and in charge. Awesome. It wants to be the cat's meow, the best thing ever. It wants that too.

But what about when the person we love doesn't want JUST us? Ouch. That is a freaking knife to the Ego. Let's look at it.

Imagine being with someone, whether now or in your past, and imagine them going off in GREAT JOY with someone else for sexual pleasure. Imagine it. Feel it. The ruffling feathers you are feeling are thousands of years of DNA punching through and thousands of years of social practice supporting it (just for the record, while reading this and editing it I had a visceral re-action, so please understand how natural that is). But, we don't live in caves anymore and the survival of the species is not in jeopardy *from outside forces*. So we don't need to keep having this reaction. We can train it out as a group. Training it out is healthy, because even if we never plan on being in a polyam-orous relationship, it is good to know that if the one we love needs us to step aside for their growth and joy, we can honor that. The best way to know for sure is to experience it.

Does that mean if we love them, we have to stay with them while they have multiple partners? NO. We don't have to DO anything that doesn't honor OUR being. But if they want to go? We certainly want to be able to let them do so with all the love and grace we would want for the person we love most.

When we can be in a relationship with someone and learn to let them do what they need to in order to be happy, then we have loosened our ego enough to trust ourselves to be a steward for someone else's growth. Our monogamy in the future **will be healthy if we can do this**. If we can trust ourselves to be able to let someone meet their needs without losing our minds, we can trust and be confident in our abilities as a loving partner.

Again, this does not mean we have to stay in an open relationship. This just means that healthy monogamy is based on desire, not control. That is the healthy removal of the Egoic Mind from the relationship process.

Does this mean that jealousy does not exist in a healthy relationship? No, of course not. We're animals and there are thousands of years of programming running through every breath we take. But we probably want to process our jealousy so that it doesn't impact our relationship negatively. We don't let jealousy dominate our mind. That's kinda the idea.

I really think everyone should experience this in youth, or at least be comfortable with the idea of an open relationship, for a few reasons.

1) *We don't know what the hell we want when we're young.*
2) *We do not have the confidence to be someone's everything.*
3) *We need to loosen the ego's grip on our relationship identity.*

But, there seems to me to be a natural time limit to polyamory in my opinion as we …

1) *Figure out what we want.*

2) *Have the confidence to be someone's everything.*

3) *Have a loosened ego so we trust that our monogamy is based on healthy desire.*

The Fit ... and Straying

The Fit of any relationship has to do with the Job of that relationship and how well the participants are getting that job done. Chapter 10 part 2 talked about being "unfuckable" ... and that is the description of what happens when the job isn't getting done.

When the job isn't getting done in a one on one relationship ... the sexual aspect goes away as the mutual respect goes away. The sex dies down, is unfulfilling, or stops altogether. That is such a waste of a perfectly good human body.

When the Straying occurs with the man ... I call it Secretary Syndrome. When it occurs with the woman I call it the Dethroned Man. In both cases, male vitality and female receptivity have diminished.

Secretary Syndrome is when we have lost the respect of our partner, or lost our self-respect, usually both, and possibly one leading to the other (this happens in lots of ways, and can happen in every partnership type). Keeping mutual respect is work, and if we can't do the "job" of the relationship, we're going to lose that.

So what happens when we've lost it in this "straying" scenario? We seek to get the respect back, BUT NOT WITH THE PERSON WE LOST IT WITH ... because that's too much work and effort (it actually may be impossible). Instead we seek out someone that we know will respect us. In general, this is someone who doesn't know our failures and thinks we're magic in some way. That's why I call it Secretary Syndrome, the *older man cheating on his wife with a younger woman version* is the perfect symbol of what this looks like. The roles of course can be changed … but looking to be respected and magic in someone else's eyes is the whole point of it, because then we can feel *vital* again.

When a woman strays, I call it the Dethroned Man, because his lack of vitality has made him a non-entity … which means that she can't be seen, heard, or felt. The sickness of a king is death to his queen, so he must be dethroned. She reaches out to replace him by being with a vital man. Then she is seen, heard, and felt again. In this way, she can exist and can survive.

Both cases can happen simultaneously, of course, and can happen in any type of monogamous relationship where the Fit isn't right and the Job isn't getting done.

But … in the case of polyamory … no one has to face the fact that they are not getting the job done. They can simply go be with someone else. See, you can't really get excited about being intimate with someone you have lost respect for, but if you can just go be with someone else … that's not even a problem. In the case of polyamory, we do not have to work as hard or succeed at healthy Interdependence to remain *sexually* vital.

This isn't a failure. Getting the "Fit" right is really rare and getting the "Job" done takes patience, focus, and years of practice. This is why I happily suggest polyamory as an awesome way to figure out *who we want to be and how we want to relate* to our partners.

The other reason I like polyamory? It DOESN'T lead to Mate Hoarding.

I'm a romantic. I like being trapped. I worked really hard to be worthy of being someone's everything (or as close to it as gets the Job done).

The world of relationships is crazy, confusing, and frustrating. I definitely suggest keeping things open and keeping the ego loose until we know exactly what we want and are willing to do *ALL that is necessary for it.*

Chapter 13:

Priceless Skills and the Speed Dating Checklist

I generally know when I'm writing the most important chapter of the book. I get excited and focused, and I don't know where to begin. I know that this will likely be the chapter the most worth re-reading, so I will do my best to make this as rich an experience for you as it is important to me.

Priceless skills in relationships. There are not too many that are specifically for couples. Most skills for couples are the general skills we need everywhere in life. Being a decent parent, roommate, friend, etc. These … are not those. These are different because the emotional complexity and sheer POWER of the human heart creates problems in relationships that simply *do not exist elsewhere*. Also, bearing the responsibility of honoring someone's heart demands a bit more from us than exists elsewhere.

The skills are …

1) Processing Emotion (for self-relating and managing behavior)
2) Wolverining (mainly for men, holding space and providing safety … as women are generally already good at *presence* and *recovery*)
3) Imaginary Friending (for patience and trust)

4) Conscious Validation Self-Talk (to keep from distracting ourselves into sabotage)
5) Taking Rejection Well (for the healthy integration of experience)
6) Opportunity Consciousness and Adjusting (for the ever-evolving needs of the relationship)
7) Gratitude and Enjoyment
8) Knowing the Speed Dating Checklist

I am going to separate these into parts, so we can focus on each one separately before seeing the kind of magic they can achieve when used together. And it is magic, in my humble opinion.

Part 1: Processing Emotion

I plan to write an entire book on Processing Emotion as my next work. It definitely *deserves* an entire book. But for now, let's just look at what it is and how to DO it (it's an action).

Below is an essay I wrote a couple years ago on the steps of processing emotion. Most of the steps seem superfluous until we really get into trying to do them. The discomfort that accompanies emotional activation is so profound that ***most of the steps are simply there to keep us from distracting ourselves away from the feelings themselves***. When the feelings do not have the audience with us that they demand, the leftover energetic frustration can have a huge effect on our daily lives.

Think of it like showering. Processing Emotion is the necessary cleansing that we need to do to keep up our Emotional

Hygiene as a human being. Maybe for a couple days we can get away with not doing it, but going longer than that is going to affect those closest to us. If we can't learn to clean areas of ourselves, they are going to rot and fester and get infected. If we're alone, this isn't a huge deal. When we are partnered, ***this is everything***.

*

We never get perfect at Processing Emotion, and that's okay. That's one of those adorably infuriating life struggles that keep adapting to keep pace with our evolving natures.

The next skill is all about "emotional recovery." We don't know how much good we do being present for someone in a time of emotional upheaval. It's a lot. It's a big deal. It can be and often is life-saving and life-changing. It is also the greatest source of intimacy and trust that can exist. Being able to take a moment with someone while they are out of control and expressing their entire selves in a brutal and vulnerable manner is the highest form of parenting and the greatest gift we can give those we are in partnership with.

But ... knowing we need to do it and *being able to do it* are two vastly different things. Here's the original essay I wrote on Processing Emotion ... I've only had to edit it a tiny bit since writing it three years ago.

*

I've written a 550-page book on Consciousness, and in the end all of what I say is geared toward one issue, and that is "processing emotion" as the primary need for the healthy operation of Consciousness, and the answer to "How do I proceed?" basically every time the question is asked.

I can only tell you that it's the most powerful tool I've found in decades of searching. It's the only thing close to freedom. It is like bottled courage, divine presence, and confidence all wrapped up into one beautiful package. Processing emotion. That's it.

Every coaching/mentoring/advice situation I'm in boils down to processing emotion ... what emotion is causing problems, and how we process it.

Every issue we have with our growth and expansion is us trying to run from processing emotion by using one of a million techniques to get away from having to sit confidently with ourselves and hold space during discomfort. Don't get me wrong, even when we are committed to this practice in such a way that it becomes a habit, it still doesn't work every time, and that is humiliating and infuriating (that's of course another reason why we do anything we can to escape having to do it).

Before I get too abstract, let's look at what processing emotion is.

1) Recognize an emotional activation. This is something that happens to us. We get emotionally activated by the world around us.

2) Feel the emotion. Sounds redundant, but most of this process is centered on staying in the emotion. Feel it. Feel its character and acknowledge how comfortable or uncomfortable we are with feeling it (this is different for every emotion and every person experiencing it).

3) SURRENDER to the emotion. Specifically STOP YOURSELF FROM RUNNING AWAY AND ESCAPING THE EMOTION. Say "This is the emotion I'm feeling, and I'm just going to sit here like a boss and feel it for a minute, or as long as I can." Resist the seductive temptation to allow the mind to steal our consciousness away from the discomfort.

4) Outlast the emotion. Nothing is permanent. It wants to trick us into believing it is, but it's not. Just hang out and the emotion will pass.

5) Learn the lesson and validate the experience. Every emotion is telling a story. When it has passed we can see what we were reacting to pretty easily. Then we take a breath … and validate what has just happened. This will give us confidence in all future moments where processing is difficult. Because "validating" is abstract until described, I'll describe it. Validating is when we recognize that the emotion has passed and that we have outlasted and learned from it, and we take a Breath of Gratitude WHILE having that recognition. That completes the experience.

There are so many mental constructs built to keep us from doing this. Entire religions are based on releasing us from being accountable for this, and they do pretty well on membership if I have my facts straight.

Free Will? If you have Free Will, you don't have to process emotion because you can just "choose" to not be influenced by unresolved emotion. Bullshit. If we don't sit with an uncomfortable emotion and stay present for its life cycle? *We have yielded our right to keep it from influencing us in the future*. If we toss our hands up and shut our eyes? *The passenger of the car takes over steering duties*. This is why we always feel like things aren't our fault. We're not steering--our unprocessed emotions are. So to us it makes sense that it's not our fault, even though that's a load of crap.

What I see everywhere is people being motivated PRIMARILY by their long history of unprocessed emotions. If we haven't processed it? It has a motivating hand in our every decision and behavior. True story.

NO ONE gets out of this. We are all living in human bodies and having a human experience. The purpose of that may or may not be "integrating momentary emotional connection and experience to find resonance and rapture" … but I think it is. And even if it's not?

Processing emotion is still our most important job.

Having issues with the spouse? Process emotion (anger, fear, resentment).

Trying to grow emotionally and expand? Process emotion (guilt, fear, doubt).

Trying to allow abundance? Process emotion (shame, self-doubt, guilt).

Trying to forgive? Process emotion (anger, fear, sadness).

Trying to feel better about your life? Process emotion (regret, shame)

Trying to be a better driver? Process emotion (road rage, dystopic distraction)

Wondering what is wrong in a certain situation? Have you processed the emotion? Odds are you haven't.

We are souls having a human experience. This is true. What we rarely say is that this human experience is simply beyond the capability of a soul to endure *even with decades of acclimation*. And rather than face this stuff head on, the manipulators and power vendors of the world realize that if they can give us a justifiable way out of this, WE WILL TAKE IT EVERY TIME. We're not cut out for processing emotions. We can pretty much trace every personal and societal issue back to this fact. No joke. I've been looking at it since I finished the book (now three years ago) and to be honest this ONE thing is …

1) The thing that souls have a hard time with doing in a human body

2) The only thing we *need* to get good at doing in a human body.

If someone comes to you with a problem … think to yourself: "What emotion is not being processed, and how can I help this person process that emotion?" (This applies to yourself also.)

Many people have asked me how I got to be where I am. Many people want to be where I am. My life is really badass. This? This is the long and short of it. There is no way around it. We cannot get to

"Peace" or "Home" without processing emotion. Why? Because the threat of having to process emotion we don't want to process is so great that *we will never feel safe if we can't do it*. EVER. We. Will. Never. Feel. Safe.

Have a feeling like heartbreak? Run toward it, or you'll be running away forever. Our HOME IS IN THE PAIN. OUR CRUMBLED BONES ARE THE FOUNDATION FOR OUR FUTURE PEACE. This is The Opportunity of our entire existence. Coming to peace through processing the chaotic emotion of this frail human body. This is "Life Purpose"-level stuff.

Safety and Home do not lie in the removal of stressors, but in the habituated ability to process them and move forward with confidence. PERIOD.

*

Yeah, re-reading that makes me happy every time.

WOLVERINE!!!

Wolverining is all about Holding Space. Holding Space is all about giving someone else the opportunity to process emotion in our presence without our reactivity affecting their process. What we need to do is recognize their activation and then trigger into a larger perspective *as fast as possible* and stay *as long as needed* during whatever activation is being handled. This means that we may end up being a target for anger transference … but in a relationship, this is a necessary sacrifice "in the moment" (stuff often gets sorted out later, as we are generally not the intended target for the activation). This is one of the main ways that we as partners can help our lovers with their previous traumas. Some of our own personal issues *may not get processed immediately* and *need to be tended to later*. But the idea is that the better we get at this, the less damage we take during the event itself. There are times now when I don't take any damage, where I would have years ago.

So, who's seen the first *X-Men*? This analogy rests on the Wolverine character, so if you haven't seen it, try and keep up.

When we first find Wolverine, we get a look at what we want our Divine Masculine, space-holding, emotional-processing selves to look like ... someone who can take beating after beating "without *losing feeling* and without *being destroyed*." For all intents and purposes, he is immortal, but not invincible. He gets hurt, and he recovers. That's the job.

"Does it hurt when they come out?" Wolverine was once asked about his retractable claws.

"Every time," he replied.

This is what we are shooting for when we hold space, especially as men. We are not going for callous or aloof or escape or logic or whatever reason we have not to show up fully. We are going for ...

1) Showing up,

2) Taking punishment and pain,

3) Not reacting negatively,

    And

4) Recovering as fast as possible without taking permanent damage.

If we do our best, over time, we end up with a pretty good Holding Space "practice." Not numb. Not callous. Just confident dealing with others' emotions with a sophisticated and elevated healing mechanism that allows everyone around us the freedom to express without our getting butthurt. This is a truly priceless skill as a lover and a parent.

There is a little extra note, though. When Wolverine was first introduced, it was before a cage fight. The guy asks the referee, "Anything goes, right?" to make sure that he could attack him in any way he pleased.

The referee says, "I wouldn't kick him in the nuts."

The guy asks, "Why?"

The ref responds, "You really don't want to piss him off."

That's the deal. Men have belts. Don't hit below them. If this happens, we may recover from the situation, but we'll build resentment. We can't help it. As in ... specifically ... there is something you can say to a man in anger that will damage his balls. This can happen to women too, of course.

We want to Hold Space. We get uncomfortable, and we recover as well as we can. Often the discomfort from the momentary activation gets processed later that day or the next. I have found luck sometimes having it go away with a good night's sleep. But the idea is that we set our own needs on the back burner for the moment during someone's activation so that they can process fully. That is Wolverining.

The third skill is much further off the norm and much less "logically" justifiable. This is also why it is one of the hardest skills to learn and why so much anxiety is prevalent at the beginning of relationships (especially as we get older and have more negative experiences to frighten us).

Imaginary Friending is LITERALLY using our imaginative strength to create something to hold on to when we lack the presence of an actual person. Why would I suggest something like this? Simple … it works.

IMAGINARY FRIENDING

Sometimes our loves are with us. Sometimes not.

Sometimes they are on a trip. Sometimes they live far away. Sometimes they are having an internal battle and are unavailable to us even though they are right beside us. Sometimes they are in a relationship with another person. Sometimes they are deployed overseas in the military. Sometimes they are incarcerated. Sometimes we haven't even met them yet. Sometimes they are not able to commit to fully being with anyone.

This can create a truly profound amount of anxiety.

Mostly when I see and work with this, it is either women waiting for men to become present in themselves for the relationship or people who are waiting to find a person they deeply connect with. Both of these situations can feel empty and hopeless. Deeply frustrating. When we are empty and hopeless, the vitality of life gets drained from us *and we cease to be fully present*. THAT MAKES THINGS WORSE.

Being drained of our vitality by uncertainty and anxiety makes it "nearly" impossible for the external reality we are presented with to change in the way we want it to. *Being hopeless makes us less capable of moving toward healthy connection.*

Quick aside … I don't believe that there is any rule saying that "when we are ready, the right person will show up." I DO think that *if we're not ready*, the right person is unlikely to see us (or we're likely to blow it). But I do not believe that we are in control of this aspect of the world. I believe that we "co-create" our destinies with many other moving pieces involved as influences.

That said … anxiety and doubt are *unsexy*. If we are anxious and not trusting, we are going to lack confidence and come off as needy. We don't attract awesome people like that, and we do not inspire presence in those we are trying to attract by embodying that. That's basic survival 101, right there. Anxiety and doubt make us unattractive.

So, what do we do?

We "create." We pretend that we are ensured success and that we basically already have the person we want, in the way we want, and that they are at their best. We lie, and believe the lie in such a way that it *keeps us secure and confident*. How do I think such a thing can work? I did it for eight years … and it kept me alive.

Now that I have used the word pretend, so that we know it is pretending, I will say the word we refer to this by. "Faith."

When it comes to believing in higher powers and ideals such as justice, having faith doesn't seem like "pretending" to us. But when we think about being with someone who is not present, and *the lack of their presence makes us suffer*, it is MUCH MORE DIFFICULT TO HAVE FAITH. So, I'm going to use the word "pretend," because it's more honest. It's more honest because having faith that someone will show up feels like a LIE when we tell ourselves.

So … if you think it will help, do it. Lie to yourself like I lied to myself. Tell yourself you truly trust, and dismiss thoughts that clash with that using Conscious Validation (we will go over that in Part 4). Then you will have the calm confidence you need to move through life and attract the people you want to.

You may be thinking to yourself, "I'm not going to do that; it's not truthful."

Okay. Feel free to embody whatever state you like. It just may not work out well for you. I work with people who battle for YEARS (yes, years) to trust in people coming through for them. What happens?

1) The lie of faith.
2) The habituation of trusting thoughts.
3) The habitual dismissal of doubt and anxiety.
4) *Actual trust* is developed over time.
5) Strength in *changing reality is achieved.*

That's how it goes down. We lie, and believe it, to weaken the dominance of our ego, which will always use our doubt to make us withdraw our hearts. We learn to not do that by forcing ourselves to do something unnatural. Then we can move forward in a way befitting a confident adult with a lot to offer. Why? *Because getting our needs met is no longer dependent on an external reality.*

There are times when it is impossible to do this, of course, times when the pain of loneliness overwhelms us. That's fine. They happen. They don't need to be the standard, though. We can generate faith and trust without evidence and live better lives as a result.

What if we trust and then are disappointed? We move on, *continuing to trust, regardless*. Why? Because it's mentally, emotionally, and physically *healthy* to do so. That's it.

I've been told after suggesting this (on a number of occasions) that it was crazy. You may be thinking it now. I will respond the way I did in those situations: *"Just try it."*

In my case, I knew my mate existed when I was fifteen. It took me twelve years to trust that she was coming regardless of the fact that I couldn't see her. Then I started getting stronger. Then I turned my life around. Then my trust in her soon-to-be presence made me confident. That confidence is what attracted her to me. It takes steps. But it works.

For many of the women I've worked with, the men they are trying to pull into presence can sense and feel the pressure of their doubts. They are less comfortable, and they stay hidden. So I tell the women to talk to them in their minds like they are there, like they aren't running from presence or hiding from intimacy. Then the women get confident. Then the man who is distant begins feeling at ease. Then the relationship gets stronger and more intimate.

There isn't a single relationship that confidence and trust can't make better.

Imaginary Friending has some bleed-over into the next section, which is based around a tool I developed and discussed in Chapter 9 of CFC101. **Conscious Validation** is a three-part practice that enables us to slowly change our thinking habits over time and keep a healthy focus during stressful moments.

Distress is prevalent in relationships because we are attached to a desired reality that we cannot control. Also, *we cannot control that attachment*, regardless of what Buddhist or New Age teachings suggest. We can battle it and we can pretend, but the need for companionship is in the species DNA. And **why should we try to control it, even if we could**? Attachment can be really rewarding. Harrowing most of the time … but rewarding nonetheless.

Distress is more of an issue in relationships (besides just being prevalent) than it is elsewhere because it is impossible to connect deeply and inspire trust when we are in states of distress. Basically put, *the stress of not being able to control a relationship can simultaneously make us incapable of strengthening it*. The other side of the coin is that it has the ability to make us stronger by inspiring us to take a more active role in our thoughts regarding the relationship, increasing our ability to trust. That is the *Opportunity* that this *distress* affords us.

As with all difficulties, they can be crippling OR empowering based on how we engage them.

Conscious Validation Self-Talk and the Flower Petals …

Conscious Validation is a process by which we refine our thoughts and thereby refine our reality. I've found that, over time, this can even change the types of thoughts we are likely to have sourcing up from our subconscious mind.

When using Conscious Validation, we must first observe. **Observation Consciousness** is vital for every aspect of life and is the first step in the process of Conscious Validation. We have to identify the "thought imprint" that we're having *in order to work with it*. If we're not paying attention or otherwise distracted, we will miss the first step.

Next, after the thought has been acquired, we decide whether or not the thought is *helpful*. HELPFUL. Nothing else matters. True/false? Doesn't matter. When we want to focus on creating a new reality for ourselves, *what is true in the present rarely represents that*, so thinking of "what is" is not very helpful for getting where we need to go. HELPFUL is the operative word.

Second, we apply the action that such a thought demands.

1) If a thought IS helpful, then we take a breath and validate it. Taking a breath while holding a thought that is helpful imprints the moment in the mind and body. This is a good thing. Thoughts that are helpful are thoughts that improve trust, self-esteem, joy, and worthiness. Thoughts about our partner that are helpful are grounded in making us feel safe, loved, joyful, and appreciated.

    We want these thoughts to be our primary thoughts during our lifetime, and for most of us, that means we have a ton of work to do to train out the other types of thoughts.

2) If a thought is "questionable," it means that there is an aspect that may work against us, regardless of how we may have intended it. Our thoughts are always open to interpretation from our conscious mind, and when we need to take an extra swipe at them for the sake of clarity and validation, we must do so.

    Questionable thoughts *need to be adjusted*. I think it's healthy to engage and adjust thoughts even when they are not obviously damaging, because as we add heightened consciousness to our internal dialogue (conscious voice and superconscious voice) it becomes easier to engage and catch ourselves in more stressful times.

Just a quick example ... "Why is he so messy?" and "Man, she's really moody" are examples of thoughts that usually get to pass through our mind without much fuss. But these thoughts over time can weaken connection, and more often, they become an area for Anger Transference to show itself. So ... we adjust.

We observe "Why is he so messy?" and adjust it to "Wow, he is so focused on what he's doing that he tends to not notice things that are trivial to him. Fascinating."

We observe "Man, she is really moody" and we adjust it to "Wow, what a varied set of emotions she is capable of processing, cool."

In both statements above, we want to move to *appreciate the differences* between ourselves and our partners. This is empowering and leaves us little room to indulge ourselves should we ever be on the borderline of allowing resentment to creep into our minds.

When we are not in a relationship (or in a very complex one), and needing to keep our self-esteem up, thoughts like "I'm too much for people," "I'm too intimidating," "I have too much baggage," and "I'm a lone wolf" are pretty common for us to say to ourselves to make us feel better about not being partnered. But we don't want those to be the truths we tell ourselves. In each case, we want to say "I am not for everyone, that's true, but I am worth it for the right person."

That's how we adjust to keep the tone we set with ourselves clear.

In all situations, if the thought does not make us more loving and confident in ourselves and for our partners (present or prospective), *it should be adjusted.*

3) Can all thoughts be adjusted if they are unhelpful? Nope.

Some thoughts are just poisonous. Some thoughts we have about ourselves or our partners are unhelpful and simultaneously so negative that they need to be outright dismissed. Not IGNORED ... DISMISSED COMPLETELY.

This means that we engage the thought by giving it an audience as we observe it, first. Then we wrap it up, take a deep breath, and cast it out (I like to think of them being shot out of a cannon, ablaze, sailing off into the distance). Then we take another breath and validate that we were *not in harmony* with the thought that was jettisoned.

Usually, the thoughts that fall under this category come in times of distress. That makes them even more difficult to dismiss, because we are super clingy and attached to our thoughts when we're emotionally activated or emotionally overwhelmed.

Thoughts like "They don't love us," "I'll always be alone," "They're just going to leave anyway, why even try?" "I'm broken and no one will ever want me," "They are just lying about everything to string me along," etc. None of those are worth arguing with. EVEN IF THEY ARE TRUE. If they are true, they still are unhelpful. Unhelpful thoughts are to be dismissed before they take a larger role in determining our behavior.

Vigilance is what it takes to be active in Conscious Validation. At my best, I run at about 50%. That means that

50% of my thoughts get checked *when I am at my most conscious.* I tend to get more aggressively thorough when I'm emotionally activated, because that's when I trust my thoughts the least.

I have noticed that when someone starts at this skill, getting from 0% to 10% is the most drastic change in their personal mindset. It is shocking how much our talking to ourselves can be damaging, and the first realizations are usually the most profound.

I have also found that anything above 0% slowly changes our lives for the better. Cool thing? When we make our mind a safer environment and empower ourselves in doing so, our partner's environment *gets safer as well.*

Conscious Validation and validating positive self-talk helps when it comes to the next part … taking rejection well.

The higher our self-esteem, the easier this is. If it's truly high and we're empowered and strong in ourselves, rejection still hurts like a son-of-a-bitch. Every. Single. Time.

How to take Rejection 101

It's not about you. The "Don't Take Anything Personally" part of the Four Agreements may not be possible to accomplish all the time, and especially not in this arena, but it's *an ideal to strive for,* isn't it?

Now, we can't help how we react to being rejected, but

we can certainly manage how we RESPOND.

Each time anyone expresses what they do or do not want, the world gets a little more refined. Each time someone decides what they do or don't want in their lives, their reality gets streamlined and opened for new opportunities as a result. This is healthy. It is healthy for us as individuals and healthy for a society to EMBRACE such expressions.

So, why can't we? Confusion around self-worth is the reason.

We mistake the temporary pangs of not being included in someone's reality, or of someone wanting to make a change regarding our relationship, as a statement about our worth. This is just a lack of sophistication in our response matrices. We can handle the momentary pain. What we can't handle is *accidentally making that pain about our worth.*

The best example, and one I wanted to cover anyway, is men engaging women in a public social setting. I have heard this complaint from women so many times that I want to highlight it here.

When a man walks up to a woman and asks her if she's interested in a talk, drink, or dance, and she says "no," men often ask "why?"

What the hell? What do they mean "why?" I didn't get this at all for many years. I had no idea why a man would ask why a woman wasn't interested. Then I realized, men believe there are certain values and standards of worth that are somehow attached to women's receptivity to us. The men who ask why are genuinely curious and confused, like they had missed some piece of a puzzle that they thought they had finished. Like ... "Hmmmm, she said no, so I must have missed something. *She should be able to tell me what it was so I can make sure it doesn't happen again.*" Then they are further confused, *even feeling betrayed* when she has no concrete answer. They mistakenly believe that there is a formula, and if they get it right, the humiliating feeling of being turned down will go away.

This is because they mistakenly believe rejection has something to do with them. They mistakenly believe that the woman assessed their being, and finding something wrong, *decided* to not like them. This is not how attraction works, fellas. It's not how reality works, either.

Reality? Reality works like this ….

We are individualized conscious beings, having been programmed by genetics and experiences over a unique lifetime, and it is unlikely that we are ever going to fit really well with anyone. That's the truth. And if we do? Nothing is promised as far as that continuing over time.

If we grow, we are likely to grow in different directions; if we are stagnant, we are likely to become disengaged and resentful. Basically 99.99% of all meetings are going to INCLUDE massive rejections of one type or another. We just have to pony up and get our little heads around that. Even with the 1/1000 or 1/1 million that we deeply mesh with there are going to be INFINITE spaces that are going to feel like rejection when we come across them.

BUT THAT IS NOT A STATEMENT ABOUT OUR WORTH. IT'S JUST A PERSONAL PREFERENCE. Good lord.

Each time someone expresses what they do or do not want, they are doing us a favor. They are helping us understand the nature of reality better. If someone rejects us for a date? They are saving us time and energy. If someone tells us they don't like something that we like, they are telling us they are not going to share in it. If someone doesn't agree with one of our deep points of view, they are telling us that they have a different value system.

All expressions of desire save time and help us refine a chaotic reality. What I started doing? I started seeing them as ALWAYS HELPING BOTH PARTIES. If I was the one being rejected, I looked for how this would help me. If I was the one rejecting, I knew that my telling the truth was sooooo much better than pretending to like something and giving the person a false sense of my reality.

The truth may not be fun for the person receiving it, but it is ALWAYS kind to the world when desire is honored. That is the Perspective that holds the most power for me regarding rejection.

The discussion above is mainly focusing on the positives of rejection, so that we can get ourselves into the proper perspective to deal with it when it happens. But I have not yet mentioned what happens as we start taking rejection more smoothly. What happens is that everything in our world gets easier. People are more at ease around us and honest with us. We become naturally more attractive to everyone.

Thus, becoming adept at handling rejection, makes us less likely to be rejected. That's just the ironic truth.

All of these abilities have one common thread. They are opportunities. Opportunity is always present. Regardless of what the situation is, the "Capital O" of opportunity is there with us. Instead of thinking of it like a concept, I have come to think of it as a living thing presenting itself to me for commune. I have sought to have the courage to reach out to it.

Thinking of Opportunity like this has changed my life.

Opportunity Consciousness

"There is something you can do … with EVERYTHING that happens to you."

This is true. There is nothing that can happen to us that we can't find a way to engage. Life is going to throw the kitchen sink at us, honestly, and how many times we can recognize the Opportunity being offered us rather than being overwhelmed will be directly proportional to how happy and strong we become as a result.

Opportunity is the difference between slavery and empowerment.

Opportunity is the difference between reaction and response.

Opportunity is the difference between our traumas making us weak and making us strong.

Opportunity is the difference between people becoming more closely bonded when times are hard or their bonds breaking.

Opportunity is the difference between resentment and understanding.

Opportunity is the difference between fostering forgiveness and being weighed down by grudges.

Opportunity is the difference between being crippled by

life and becoming refined by life.

It is the one tool that can be used at any time. All we have to do is ask *"What is the Opportunity here?"* Sometimes doing this is impossible. I am not going to tell someone who has just been handed a divorce or lost a child that it is an Opportunity. *I am not going to say that.* But that doesn't mean it isn't an Opportunity, and it doesn't mean that allowing ourselves to focus on what Opportunity it may hold can't help us. It *always* can.

Opportunity Consciousness is a Perspective that can empower us and change our lives just by thinking about it. Allowing ourselves to see where we could grow and learn from a difficult situation *takes the power away* from the brutal world that hurt us and *puts energy into the immortal soul that fuels us.* Just asking the question … "What is the opportunity here" … is a transcendent maneuver by the human conscious-ness into a greater realm of accountability and empowerment.

Just ask. Watch where it takes you. Watch what answers show up to inspire you forward. Thinking in terms of Opportunity and embodying Opportunity Consciousness changes the way our mind works to face incoming trials and problems.

How does this apply to relationships? It makes facing life's battles much more bearable if we know we are not going to have our partners bail on us. Being a person who turns tough situations into opportunities to grow and move forward is in-spiring. I want to be that, and I want to be around people that do that.

Do you want to be around people who see difficulties as opportunities? Do you want to be someone who sees the world like that? Ask the question. That's all it takes.

"What is the Opportunity here?"

One of the issues that gets a lot of air time in circles where mindfulness is employed is "Gratitude." This is a vital part of any relationship, but the most important aspect of showing and embodying Gratitude is often missed ... that aspect is *enjoyment*.

The people we are in close contact with (especially our mates) all have skills and qualities that are specific to them. It is not that we must be grateful for them *by recognition alone*, but that we must actually *use and enjoy them*.

The Husband and the Cake from CFC 101 ...

The following is an excerpt, mildly edited, form CFC101 that references enjoyment in relation to manifestation. But rather than a relationship with the Universe, I am suggesting that relationship exists between ourselves and our Divine Other.

*

I have wondered about aspects of the Law of Attraction since the first time I heard Abraham Hicks when I was about eleven. I knew that some people were simply better at it than others, and recently I have realized why. Dream, delight in the dream, and allow the dream. Be gracious for it when you get it ... NOT ENOUGH. I realized one word has been missing from the process to make it a complete exchange ....

"The last prerequisite for manifestation is that you VALIDATE the exchange and connection by ENJOYING the manifestation."

Allow, be gracious, sure … that's a start. But the next example will show you why that's simply not enough for universal discourse to occur and intervene for the fulfillment of your yummy requests. It is the husband and wife drama … the wife's birthday.

Wife is craving a chocolate birthday cake (homemade delicious gooey chocolate), and she mentions it enough so that the husband realizes she really would love it as a gift. The husband gets all the ingredients and works with his dearest love to make and deliver the cake, which is presented on the birthday at the appropriate moment.

The wife thanks him profusely and showers him with affection. But … she refrains from eating the cake.

A week goes by and she doesn't touch it. The husband ends up throwing it out.

She asked for the cake, she allowed the cake, and she was grateful for the cake … but … she didn't eat it.

Assume you're the husband. The next time she asks for something, are you as motivated to act? I'm not. I wanted to see her face light up when she tasted it and I'm disappointed that I did not get to have that experience. I don't want to be upset about it, but I am. In this situation, a piece of the exchange was missing. Because of that, the exchange was not *validated*.

We are all the wife in this situation. The husband's role is being played by the Universe. We need to eat the cake. Otherwise, in the same way the husband feels dejected, the Universe does not get its vibration matched.

What the world wants from us is the Vitality Gasp of enjoyment. That is the fulfillment of the cycle. The world doesn't want a thank-you card. I say the world, rather than the Universe, because ALL conscious beings respond to the Vitality Gasp. A baby laughing, a lion roaring, a wolf howling, love at first sight, the jump from the ledge into the ocean, deep sexual satisfaction, triumph, any mind-blowing experience, the first bite of a delicious piece of cake ... these are what we ALL live for.

Those who enjoy life the most, in my experience, seem to have their dreams fulfilled at ease, without worry. And when their dreams are fulfilled, *they love up on them.*

*

What we want to glean from this, in reference to our Divine Other, is that the amazing qualities embodied by the one we love, the ones that garnered our attention and led to our attraction ... we need to ENJOY those aspects of our partner. We need to enjoy them.

It's as if the wondrous qualities of the person we are in union with are a wondrous garden that *needs our loving attention and adoration to be nourished.*

The best parts of who we are? We want our partners to BASK in those ... we want to see the shine of our brilliance reflected in the loving adoration of our Divine Other.

Enjoyment completes the cycle of manifestation by validating the satisfaction of desire. Enjoyment also fuels the constant motion of a relationship as it continuously births itself into the future.

I split this chapter up because I know I'm going to have to refer back to it over the course of my life to focus on specific skills with people as they face different obstacles. The final section of this chapter is what we want to be able to KNOW TO ASK at the outset … so that we may waste the least amount of time in situations that are not good fits.

The Speed Dating Checklist

Let's say we have five minutes to figure out if someone can handle a relationship. There are ways to figure this out. It's not magic.

What I have found is that people generally don't ask direct questions. There are many ways people try to go about figuring whether someone is relationship material or not, mostly emotional games built on sabotage and manipulation. Those not only undermine trust by being indirect, but they are unlikely to yield direct conscious answers to our questions.

So, I figured I'd just find the questions and make a list that would work for anyone. Most of them are simply to make the person think of answering a question they may not have ever had to answer for themselves. Some are useful far beyond that, though.

1) Do you more habitually resist, repress, or process your emotions?

2) What emotion do you least like to feel?

3) How well do you adjust to changes, trivial or life-altering … both?

4) When are you most irritable?

5) How have your relationships up until now helped make you who you are? How is your relationship with your exes?

6) Do you want a relationship like your parents, or not? Whether so or not, what did you not like about theirs?

7) What bad habits are you engaged in changing for yourself on the daily?

8) How do you handle guilt on a scale of 1-10?

9) Are the needs of the person you're in a relationship with a stressful burden to you, or an opportunity for you?

10) How is your behavior when you are hungry, angry, or tired?

11) How volatile are your breakups usually?

12) On a scale of one to ten, how well do you take care of yourself?

13) Are you willing to Parent me a little if I need it, on the promise that I will do the same for you if needed? Yes or no?

IF THEY ARE DIVORCED WITH KIDS *

14) How do you honor the mother/father of your child?

15) How do you process any resentment that comes from that relationship?

16) How do you help make sure the mother/father of your child is comfortable so they can do the best for your child when they are the lead parent?

17) If your ex was giving you zero support and tons of grief, could you still give 100% to them for the sake of your child?

So ... how did you do on these? You're not supposed to do great. It's supposed to be a difficult set of questions, because life is a difficult thing. We aren't going for survival of the species here. We're going for happiness. We're going for synergy. We're going for union. We're going for *something new*.

My guess is that just asking these questions will alter the level of awareness and respect in the relationship from the outset as well as providing a healthy vocabulary in it going forward. My guess is also that in seeing and answering these for yourselves that you will come away with more respect for the deep challenges that arrive with every relationship we get into.

Since this was my brilliant idea ... I'll show everyone where I was when Claudia and I met by answering the questions from that point of view.

1) Processing mostly, but I have a ton of anger and frustration that gets to me daily.

2) Anxiety then. It's rare now. (Now anger is my most discomforting.)

3) I don't do well with trivial changes; I do really well with large ones.

4) When I'm hungry. I lose my mind when I'm hungry. It's a mix of low blood sugar and the meds I take.

5) They showed me what I was good at, and what I wasn't very good at. They also showed me a lot of what I didn't want from myself or another person. My relationship with some of them is good, but all have some amount of respect.

6) Yes, for the most part--my mom and stepfather, that is. They couldn't sustain it, though. That's what I would like to improve on.

7) Handling anxiety better, specifically not having to get drunk every night to get through the day.

8) I don't handle guilt so well. It makes me really uncomfortable, so I am very careful with my behavior so as not to incur it.

9) I love them. I love intimate weirdness and challenges. I love investigating and figuring stuff out about the person I love; it's exciting to me in a way nothing else is. It's like being a pioneer.

10) Oh, goodness. Not good. Irritable, impulsive, rebellious, and shitty. Not eating or sleeping when I need to makes my bipolar manic stuff kick in and I can act like a jerk. I have really started to focus on making sure this doesn't happen, though.

11) Not bad in comparison to what I've seen from others. I am not an unkind person, so being mean or vengeful doesn't come into play. I'm too sensitive and empathic, and again, I really dislike feeling guilty.

12) Goodness, tough question. I work on it a lot, and I have gotten so much better at it. But I am honestly a freaking mess. And while I'm active and engaged in my well-being all day, I still tend to get overwhelmed and what I do still tends to not be enough. That's just the truth.

13) I'd be honored.

14-17) I haven't experienced these.

I didn't just fill out the checklist because I wanted to add pages to this book. I did it because it should be known that having sparkling-pretty answers to these questions does not mean someone is ready. It likely means they have rehearsed and are putting a shine on. It should look messy when someone answers these questions, as that means that they **are aware of their own mess**. That's much more important than not having a mess.

Why is being aware of and working with our mess better than not having a mess? Because life CREATES messes … it just does. There are going to be messes, regardless of how clean our past has been. We want someone aware and well-practiced at "messy," otherwise, how will we depend on them when "messy" arrives?

I was a mess, and honestly, I still am a mess. I just work every day on it.

The idea I've found to be prevalent is the idea that "mastery" leads to a certain level of "cleanliness." That *expectation* leads to **a lot of bad relationship choices**. In actuality, it is a "willingness" to adjust to discomfort and do the work with the reality we're presented with that creates "cleanliness" in a relationship. *There is no substitute for that, period.*

The skills in this chapter can change every aspect of our lives. Even if they lead to endless frustration in dating or partnering, they will improve our ability to experience joy and live fully.

If there is nothing else in this book you care about reading? I still suggest reading and re-reading this chapter, as well as sharing it with others. I can testify, as a counselor of men and women in relationships, that each of these skills has come up as a solution to frustrations in relationships (especially those mental battles we have with ourselves about how we should be behaving).

Do they guarantee anything? Just that engaging them will make you a better person. That's not so bad, I don't think.

Chapter 14:

Stupid Questions:
Understanding Biological Imperatives

"Why aren't people that aren't me, more like me? I don't understand why it makes sense for them to _____."

This is what almost every one of the questions in this chapter boils down to. People are different. I am going to generalize for the sake of saving time and addressing the largest number of *major* issues as quickly as I can, but truly, everyone is really different.

Most of the differences between the sexes and divine energies boil down to ingrained "survival of the fittest" programming that was ground into our DNA over the past 100,000 years or so. This is why humans still have many Biological Imperatives functioning as *highly powerful motivators* within their behavioral matrices.

When we get into a situation where we can't understand someone's behavior, it can lead to a huge amount of frustration and resentment. We tend to think they are trying to mess with our peace of mind on purpose. This is inaccurate, of course, and can be tragic if we don't figure out what is going on. If we take a moment to understand why there is a real difference in programming, we can get on with our lives without being so affected by frustration.

These are the questions I've found to be the most prevalent ... one by one. Each one will get their own section. I do suggest sharing these, too, especially with your kids as they grow into adulthood. Biological Imperatives are not going anywhere until we can engage them at an early age. Even if we get to a spot where we are consciously able to work with these, there are still plenty of imperatives that showcase skills and strengths we don't necessarily want to do away with.

Taking these issues to heart and working with them together can also create a level of trust in a union that is truly powerful.

Why are women always trying to change us?

This is the Divine Feminine. Don't get all bunched up about it. Women do it with friends, family, and all the time with their mates. The ability to adjust and adapt, as well as the need to continue pressing forward in this area, is a part of the feminine survival matrix. It doesn't mean we're not good enough. It means she loves us. *It's her version of the protection instinct*. The more we are capable of adapting, the more comfortable we will be.

So, she's going to force us to adapt over and over again forever. That's just how it goes. It won't stop unless she doesn't give a shit about us anymore.

This can exist in men and women, of course, but it is the natural instinct of the Divine Feminine. Agents carrying out this message will likely all have different delivery methods, so don't expect consistency.

Why is he so uncomfortable with emotion, especially mine?

This is another survival issue. Another Biological Imperative (getting sick of that term yet?). This also falls under the umbrella of protection. The Divine Masculine has learned how to manage emotion a little. Those still working to gain ground in their emotional reality, or those who are completely unaware, are going to have serious issues here. Knowing why they have those issues should help take a little pressure and frustration out of the situation.

When a woman or child is emotionally distressed, the man in the situation is going to be seriously upset. This is not *just* because they are empathic, it is because they are natural protectors. The instinct of men, upon seeing any attack, is to neutralize the threat and create safety. When the discomfort comes from emotion, the attack is coming from INSIDE THE HOUSE (cue scary music). How are we supposed to protect you from something that is attacking you from the inside? How are we supposed to fulfill our genetic instinctual mandate? HOW!? It scrambles our brains.

As an added bonus, when we can't create safety and neutralize the attacker with our instinctual brute force, we start feeling shame. So, when we are confronted with an emotional distress reaction, we feel empathy, frustration, guilt, and shame. We have failed as men, as providers and protectors, and we are useless as human beings and should be shunned. Maybe that seems a tad drastic, but that's what survival programming does until we engage it and begin to unwind it.

So, what needs to happen? What needs to occur to get from here to where we want to be?

We need to replace the idea of "attacking and neutral-izing a threat" with "holding space for processing." The pres-ence of an emotion, while a threat to the masculine psyche, is actually the best OPPPORTUNITY a man has to *provide safety*. Instead of attacking the emotion, it is his job to just sit there while the emotional response takes place, without run-ning away or getting overwhelmed by the feelings he is hav-ing about it. That is the job of protecting in the NOW.

This is NOT easy. It's not easy for a number of reasons, but most often it is because there is a decent amount of chaotic volatility being expressed, and he may have to take a couple bullets for the team. But, *as long as he knows it's for the team*, the union, he's much more likely to take them … and taking them is how the present-day Divine Masculine protects his mate and children from threats.

Guys, the emotions pass, and they hurt only a little. Just hold space.

"Why are women so crazy?"

This one may ruffle some feathers, but it's a question I've taken many times over the years, so I am going to honor it in this book (remember the chapter title). Also, for every man I've had ask this question, I've had a mother tell me they were so happy they had a boy so they wouldn't have to deal with an insane teenage girl.

When I was a young boy and growing into being a young man, I had many mythical pictures of this creature, woman. She was a servant of life, and the very essence of the Universe flowed through her body to create more consciousness and vitality. She was a princess and maiden gloriously tied to becoming a mother and sacrificing her old self to the future of humanity, shedding her views of self to take on larger and larger roles within the community. She was a magic vessel of joy to be enjoyed, honored, and served so that the greatest amount of pleasure and richness could be experienced by all that came within reach of her bountiful glory.

All of that is true. 100% true. But that's not what it looks like … even if we know that's what it is.

Her body is in service of the Universe; so is her emotional body. The emotional reality is built to serve the survival of the species. Her ability to attach to a child or a mate is higher and deeper than any correlative could do justice to. Her ability to bear and forget pain, unreal. Her mood swings and desires, beyond measure. Her wrath, boundless. Her needs, conflicting and impossible to meet, for more than a temporary split second. Her logic, in service of other processes. Her intuition, powerful.

The result of these mixes of motivations and realities is oddly simple. Woman is a conscious being, who, regardless of all the awful shit going on in the world, is still so passionate about life that she is willing to carry a defenseless growing being inside her body and share her nutrition with it, then devote her life to raising it until it is ready to fend for itself.

Why are women so crazy? **So that the freaking species doesn't die out**. It's a Biological Imperative to have some irrationality at the foundation and imbalance everywhere else … because the proposition of life vs. pain is not honestly one I'd think any man would make. She's crazy, because **someone has to be in order for there to be world**.

Don't just cut her some slack. ***Get it***. Get that her wild-ness is actually what we want, *rather than just something we are willing to overlook*. If you don't want that? That's fine. I just have found that anyone who understands, sits with, and embraces it has a lot more fun. Your choice.

One more thing. It's not that this is a picnic for women, either. Both men and women have similar gripes about the chaos of the feminine emotional matrix. Why is it that I focus on a man's ability to change his perspective on this? Because unlike a woman, a man can just walk away from the chaos, while a woman has to live with it inside of her … unrelenting and exhausting.

Just like a child. I don't want men walking away from ei-ther; it makes for a crappy world.

Why don't men notice anything/Why are women picky about cleanliness and appearance?

This is a more in-depth answer, because it actually cor-relates to some hardware differences in the brain, specifically the hippocampus and amount of grey matter vs. white mat-ter. I am going to go a step further to highlight something I believe is a difference between men and women (generally, *not every single person*), and then show how it is a Biological Imperative honed over thousands of years that we can now choose to embrace *rather than getting upset about it*.

Men are hunters, women are nesters. Yes, it's a general-ization. I'm aware. But over the hundreds of thousands of years it took us to move from caves to condos, some specific hardware differences have emerged. These changes are in the area of attentive focus. Why have a pairing between individuals if everyone could do everything equally? *Doesn't make sense for survival*.

Men are generally linear thinkers (more white matter). They can focus and hone in on what they are looking for … and HOLD their attention really well on that one thing. They also have a list of priorities that they allow their attention to wander over. This is because they don't want bears to eat their family. But it's going to be the reason he doesn't notice when there's a small mess in the living room or why he doesn't even see your hair, much less notice your haircut.

"How could he not notice?"

Easy--*it wasn't a threat to anyone's safety, and it wasn't food*. Men have to *train* themselves to expand their attention to include non-survival-based things. They have to *train* themselves to widen their gaze. For some men this is easier than for others. This isn't lack of care; it's Biological Imperative. If a man doesn't work to widen his gaze to accommodate his woman's joys, *then THAT is lack of care*.

When I think of myself and how bad I am at widening my gaze (especially if I'm nervous or hurried), I realize how much energy and calm it takes me to relax and use some common sense. One of my favorite little anecdotes is on coffee. I wanted a cup of coffee. I went to the Keurig brewing machine to grab a single-serve cup, but they weren't there on the counter. I froze. I not only didn't start slowly looking in other areas for it, I forgot everything that was going on for the entire day.

Why? Because of **the Ladder**. The Ladder is the linear operational tool I use to get through my day, and everything I am going to do correlates to a rung on the Ladder. I get from one rung to another. If I lose a rung and am calm … I can generally replace it or move on. If the Ladder gets interrupted and I am not at my best, the loss of one rung can cost me 20-30 minutes of trying to figure out what on Earth I'm supposed to be doing.

So imagine me, *standing like a broken robot* in front of the coffee machine. Picture me totally lost, barely knowing my name. Then picture my mate walking up behind me and saying, "Oh my God, you're broken. Honey, you came in here for coffee, and it's in the cupboard right in front of you. You couldn't see it because it's not on the counter." She fixed my Ladder. And to be honest, no, *I had no idea to look in the cupboard*. That wasn't where the coffee goes (in my mind), and to expand the "coffee resting place" section of my mind I had to stop and manually make space like I was moving boxes around. This is how my brain works.

My brain is built for the efficient use of mental energy. It is built to go from one rung to the next. The ladders that are used to perform daily routines and activities were built over the length of my life. Each day when ladders get built, I try to be conscious of them in case there needs to be an adjustment. If there is an adjustment made, it's going to be a stressful few minutes that I'm going to need to process the loss and re-evaluate my priorities. This is just my brain. It is what allows me to do most of the awesome things I'm good at, but it doesn't do to well with adjustment. I've had to learn that, and it hasn't been easy.

Why have I had to learn it? Because women are abstract thinkers, and being around my mate means I'm going to have to adjust all the time.

This gets me to why women are concerned with

appearance and cleanliness. Biological Imperative. They are not focused on one thing (like bear attacks); they are responsible for *the entire inside of the cave*. They are responsible for health and care. This means that their attention has to be widened ... because anything that is even *the slightest bit out of place is a threat*. It doesn't have to be bear-sized.

Every person has a standard of cleanliness. Not an "expectation," but a threshold. This threshold, once crossed, applies a large amount of stress to the human mind. For women, their widened gaze makes it much more difficult ever to be at peace with the cleanliness of the space they live in.

When men and women are living together and sharing space, these minor quibbles can turn into areas where resentment can get stored through repeated frustration. It can destroy trust. This is what I am trying to put a stop to by describing this.

Men are not careless; they are just built differently. Women are not trying to interrupt your flow and nag you; they are built to care about subtleties, and they have no idea that you are halfway up one ladder when they bring you a task or focus point.

Men and women cannot imagine what each other are like. The goal is to slowly learn thinking styles from each other so that each can become more adept at living, in general. And again, this is, *in general*. Many women and men have lots of different thinking types. The point is that *we do not want to assume carelessness or disrespect* on behalf of our partners when it is likely a structural difference being expressed. What we do want ... is to learn everything we can about the people we share space and love with.

In the end, almost all of loving is connected to learning. This is how the feeling of love translates into being able to *honor* that love through useful thought and action.

In Coffee for Consciousness 101, I spent an entire chapter on the "blessing" of being able to love to show the difference between the *virtuous acts* of honoring love and the *basic feeling* that hopes to inspire those actions.

The feeling is only the spark. Any healthy fire needs wood and careful tending. That is much more than any one spark could provide.

Chapter 14 Part 2:

EQUALITY ... Not to Be Confused With SAMENESS

There is an uncomfortable aspect of talking about male and female, masculine and feminine, that I am going to address now at the end of this chapter. For many reading this, it may be an obvious truth. For those that are struggling with the differences I am pointing out between men and women, and masculine and feminine energy (which exist within all and are not gender based), this is just a little reminder about the nature of equality.

Equality does not mean "sameness."

It doesn't.

Men and women don't have to be the same to be equal. Arguing that men and women are the same ... or that they SHOULD be the same ... is freaking ridiculous and disrespectful. Why is it disrespectful? Because when anyone argues that men or women should be _____ (fill in any blank) they are basically saying "The world and people should be how I think they should be."

I have a hard time tolerating disrespect like that. I have a harder time responding to it in a peaceful fashion. The audacity of one conscious being feeling so "in the right" about how things should be that they feel comfortable stepping on someone else's sovereignty is *unnerving* to me.

I'm sure there are a couple thinking: "Yeah, but you just told people for the past hundred pages how you think they should be, isn't that hypocritical?"

But … I didn't. I have been saying, and will continue saying, "If you want a healthy happy relationship, then this perspective is a good idea to have and these are good tools to use." IF. That's a BIG "IF."

Men and women are different. Masculine and feminine energy are different. I'll go further … everyONE is different. EveryTHING is different. I'm not bringing revelations forward here. But regardless of everyone being different, equality exists. *Equality exists as a **value we assign** to the **respect we give** to conscious beings*. For that, it doesn't matter if we're from Mars and Venus … or from the Bronx and the beach. It doesn't.

People are different. Men and women are different. We're still equal. We all have the opportunity to grow and parent others, help, be kind, love, and be loved. We respect *that*. We honor it.

IT'S ALL IN YOUR HEAD! Upgrading the Golden Rule.

The reason that people being different is frustrating to many of us is that if someone is different from us, then we cannot expect them to behave as we see fit. If they are the same, then we can judge them, make decisions on their behalf, make assumptions about them, etc. Lots of fun things for our ego to get all hot and riled up about.

Also, if someone is the same as us, then we don't have to do any investigating to find out how they are different. Much more, we don't have to be accountable for treating them APPROPRIATELY. We can just treat them the way we would treat different versions of ourselves.

But they aren't different versions of us. They are separate.

"Do unto others as you would have them do unto you."

"Treat others the way you want to be treated."

Those can be twisted. They can be twisted and bastard-ized to give people a false rationale. They can be twisted to mean "If I like something ... then I can do it to everyone."

I love peanut butter, but that does not mean I am going to give it to my son, who is allergic.

I love loud music, but that does not mean I am going to play it in the car for my friend who has a headache.

I love contact sports, but that does not mean I am going to tackle strangers.

I love being alone when I'm upset, *but that does not mean I abandon my mate when she is.*

And these people being different from me does not make us not equal. We're not supposed to be the same.

This is where those that give advice (professionally or not) sometimes get into trouble. They make the incorrect assump-tion that the same motivating factors and machinery are work-ing within each individuated human being.

How many times have you heard "It's all in your head"?

I've heard it hundreds of times. Therapists, friends, lovers.

What does it mean, though?

It means "What you are having an issue with is not an is-sue for me, *so it must not be a real issue for you.* Therefore, I'm not going to address it seriously."

Awesome. Thanks for that.

Unfortunately, I wasn't like my therapists. My mind and chemistry were different from theirs in ways they couldn't imagine. That's okay. That's how therapists have been taught for the most part. Emphasis on "have," and "for the most part."

We're going to change that. We're going to allow people to be different. We're going to allow them their experience of reality without trying to bend it into something that makes sense to us so that we can be more comfortable. We're going to listen, and learn, and accept someone else's truth ... even if it makes us uncomfortable. We're not going to get frustrated and bail on the situation because it's foreign. We're going to stick it out ... and in doing so we're going to LEARN.

We're not going to say things like "they're just crazy" if they have emotions or sensitivities that we don't.

We're not going to say "They just don't care" if they have odd ways of showing affection or don't notice all of the things that we do for them.

We're not going to say "They're weak willed" if they have struggles with panic, or addiction, or anxiety.

We're not. Not because we're being nice ... but because THOSE THINGS AREN'T TRUE. Pretending they're true means that everyone is the SAME ... and oddly? If everyone really were the same ... no one COULD be equal. Because then we would all be judged on the same scale that's in all of our heads.

It's time we put this old paradigm monster of judgment to bed. It may even be time to change the golden rule.

Maybe the Golden Rule of Parenting? How about that for an idea?

"Do unto others as you would have them do unto your children."

How's that for a game-changer? Certainly shows how serious I am when I speak of the need to Parent others when possible and necessary, doesn't it?

Most of my complaint in everyday life is that the masculinized world of logic does not accept the feminine world of chaos and emotion. This occurs within ALL of us ... not just between men and women (or men and men, women and women, etc.). Why is it the masculine that has the issue? Because of the nature of masculine energy. It is not about allowing. It is about protecting. The feminine is about allowing.

So, when we get into "allowing" other people to be different than we are, we start getting tied in knots in our masculine mind. This makes the egoic masculine ... the masculine *that has not integrated his feminine*, really uncomfortable. The masculine stiffens. The masculine does not want to allow this foreign idea. So ... it pretends the feminine is the same as it is, then assumes it is TOO WEAK TO PERFORM CORRECTLY. It assumes that the feminine is the same, just weaker ... *rather than allowing it to be truly different*. Beyond rude.

In general, the feminine is performing a needed creative function ... the kind of function that births new realities into existence.

But the masculine *can't see it unless it has integrated the feminine*. It can't see it because it would have to recognize and allow a reality that is beyond control or understanding. This is the ultimate of egoic disrespect. And on a cultural level throughout most of the world, this is the "norm."

So, in case it is still tough to see that people are different, let's just look at the two major sub-groups of human beings, men and women.

Nope. They're different. Sorry.

Here are some basics.

Women have periods, babies, vaginas, and breasts (and breast cancer). Their main reproductive hormone is estrogen rather than testosterone. Women are "generally" smaller in stature and carry much less lean muscle mass.

We notice that Olympic sports separate the male and female athletes, right?

Those are the "physical" attributes. Kinda hard to disagree with those, since you can see them. But what about the mental, emotional, and spiritual differences? Are we just going to ignore those BECAUSE THEY ARE INVISIBLE? REALLY? What kind of garbage is that? How does anyone think it serves them, or mankind, to ignore something integral about ourselves just because we can't see it?

Men and women have different chemistry. Different brain structure. Different means of expressing and processing emotion. Different mental focuses. Different natural talents.

If your experiences have not shown you this, I get it. I hear you. But … since some people really may need you to understand what they're saying when they say that men and women may be different, I invite you to please use Google to investigate "Differences in men and women." It may help you get some perspective that you can use, regardless of whether you believe it or not.

What I'm getting to is that equality is built on the idea that we are ALL NOT THE SAME. Equality means that we learn and adjust for the exact parts of ourselves that make us different. Equality means that we understand and ACT ON this depth of individuality that exists within all of us.

Saying someone should be a certain way is NOT equality. It is discrimination. If we were all treated the same? ALL would be discriminated against in one way or another, and each to more or less a degree. Equality can exist only in the conscious movement to allow others to be who they are, and learn from observing them. THAT is equality. THAT is what we're after. THAT is enriching to the soul of the world. THAT is kind to the myriad of differences that are birthed through each of us onto this plane ...

Equality ... not sameness.

Chapter 15:

Mitigation

The Biological Imperatives that drive a lot of our actions, specifically those that can be confusing to our partners, are not going anywhere. We need to understand them and allow some space for them to exist … hopefully without driving us completely batty.

But now that we know they exist, it's not like we're just going to let them exist within us without trying to make it a little easier on each other, are we?

"Hey, I know this is a part of things I don't get about you, but can you maybe tone it down just a tad?"

We can all get better at everything. We may not be able to eradicate our issues, or control them, but we definitely can do our best to work with them in the way that creates the most harmony for our relationship.

Note: this may be a reallllllllllllllllllly slow process.

So, since this is a little touchy, I'll just use myself as an example.

How long, as a child, did it take me to learn to put the toilet seat back down after using the bathroom? How long did it take AFTER I started focusing on it? It took me about three years. I was really trying to remember and be courteous. So, after a while, I did actually achieve my goal.

How long did it take me to learn to not raise my voice to my mother? When I turned thirteen, my voice dropped deeply and got really loud. I had gone from being a kid to being a scary adult- sounding person without knowing it. To me, I was speaking normally. To my mother, I was brutalizing her. That evolution was two years. Two years for me to drop the volume a bit.

The issues listed above are basic examples of growing up. They are *not as strong* as Biological Imperatives. They took **years**. Yes, I was a juvenile at the time, but I was conscious and aware. And really, *who says that adults are anything more than big juveniles* when it comes to managing emotional realities?

As an adult in a relationship, there are so many differences between myself and my mate when it comes to the little things. Cleanliness is a big one. She's not overly critical or a neat freak, not by any stretch of the imagination. She likes things picked up and put away … *or she can't relax.* That's not her fault. She didn't choose that reality within her. It's the nesting aspect of the feminine. So I can think to myself "Well, she's nuts. That's her issue." Or I can think to myself "Alright, I may not be good at focusing on what she is seeing that bothers her, but I bet I can get better at it over time if I try."

THIS IS ALL ANYONE IS ASKING. Make a freaking effort … an honest one. How do we know if it's an honest effort? *It should make us a little uncomfortable.* Being slightly uncomfortable in this aspect of life is a sign of refinement. It's not a bad thing.

As a result of this effort on my part, I have figured out that I tend to leave shoes and mail and water bottles and coats and pens and envelopes and papers … just about everywhere. I also have a tendency to just leave food out of the fridge for no apparent reason. Also, for a long time I left much of my clothing out, closet doors open, and folded laundry left on top of the chest rather than put away. Why? If I can't see it, it simply doesn't exist. True story.

So how do we work on all of that? Slowly and creatively.

I got better at the general littering by stopping and observing the room I was in, while pretending I was my mate. Just stopped, and looked around. Soon, things started to stick out and I could understand what she was seeing that was causing her discomfort. Leaving food out of the fridge? Yeah, I'm still bad at that. But hey, it's only been five years of living together. Yes … that was a bad joke.

In the case of the clothing, I found a better way. I found an accessory that sits on top of the chest and is open so I can see all of my clothes. This way it is "put away" and "visible" at the same time, satiating both of our natural drives for how we want things.

The issues listed above are the easy ones. Emotion reactions are the difficult ones.

I am of the mind that men and women have a completely different threshold of emotions. This has gotten me in plenty of fights, so I am going to tread softly. The fact that there may be a different *threshold* for each, and a different *activity level* for each, does NOT mean that the DEPTH of feeling for each can be assigned. And, **of course**, men may have higher activity than some women, and vice versa.

So, rather than try to make a claim that will get me tarred and feathered, I am just going to describe my mate and myself. If this is relevant to you, great.

My mate, sweet caring woman that she is, is always in a state of emotional activation. There is always a litany of emotional realities existing within her and influencing her consciousness. For me? Nope. Not at all. I am generally experiencing zero activation. This looks like it's a good thing for me, and certainly it is most of the time. But what it means … is that emotional activation, when it happens, is WAY more violent for me than it is for her. She is like a ball in a pinball machine, bouncing around. I am like a serene crane sleeping while standing on one leg. It doesn't help matters here that I am a Pisces and she is a Gemini (check Chapter 17 for more on this).

When our worlds mix? Ohhhhhh, goodness. One decent shot, and it's like I got walloped with a wrecking ball. It's shocking, stunning, and completely violent. That is what she deals with ALLLLLLLL DAY. But I'm *not used to it*, so it is really jarring.

Now we're in a weird spot. Does she hide her emotions from me to protect me? She is going to feel guilty when I get activated and affected. Then I'm going to feel guilty naturally because she was just trying to share some of her world, and my body couldn't handle it easily. This becomes a pretty nasty spiral and can lead to paralysis, *unless we are willing to work with it and get better at it.* We know this exists because we understand the emotional Biological Imperatives. She is going to get overwhelmed by emotion and need to vent rather than lose her mind, and I am going to be thrown off and feel invaded and assaulted by what's going on within her. **That is just life.** Now, what we do with it? That is EVERYTHING.

We know we're trapped by these imperatives … but their severity and their cyclical nature can be adjusted over time. I can literally tell you that the dialogue and download that would happen between us used to take 2-3 days to work itself out, and now it can work itself out in 5 sentences (sometimes). Usually we're still at it for hours when it comes to bigger stuff, but we each understand how the other works and how to make the process *as easy as possible.* I cannot begin to describe how much this knowledge matters, and how much trusting that our partner is working on their end matters.

I CAN say how delicious and delightful it is to validate the slow changes in communication over time as they occur.

When there are conflicts of this confusing nature, it is like we have to play out some weird dance and drama to get through it. Over time … we get really good at the dance. It may still not make a lick of sense to either one of us WHY it has to happen that way, but *that doesn't really matter to us as long as it works* and we get through it.

Because this is an area I believe most couples experience conflict in, I am going to describe a couple push/pull facets of MY relationship. I have seen these aspects in the relationships of others, but again, I am in no mood to assume that everyone has these issues. If you do, this will serve as a great example to work with. If not, you get to be privy to our problem-solving processes where our specific individuated natures do not exactly line up within our relationship.

Nesting/Resting and Ladder/Non-Sequitur ... Understanding Respect

In the section above I gave a few examples of how I responded to my mate's nesting drives and began to respect and understand them as a result of that effort. I did not go into deep detail about my "resting" drive. My inability to see things the way she does sources from my body's natural process of using energy efficiently. Energy is a premium to my masculine Sun self, and I organize my life in such a way as to maximize its usage. This means that when I rest ... I am completely resting. My mate doesn't have that feature built in.

When I sleep, I need a certain amount to be able to function properly. I am bipolar, I take some sleep meds, and as a result of that I need 8-9 hours a night. That's a lot, I know, don't tease. I can sleep less, of course, but I won't function optimally and therefore my energy will not be at 100% or used efficiently throughout the day. My mate not only respects that reality after testing it for a year or so, but she has begun to understand the whole of the structure in a larger sense. This brings us to projects that we take on together.

When I am working on a project, I am in "go" mode. This means that my energy is like that of an automobile. The gas is running with high RPMs at all times until the trip is over. For me to turn the car off and restart it is really difficult, sometimes not doable at all. So, I keep the engine running. This means that during the creative phases of changing around our son's room, I have to leave or find something menial and tedious to do to "keep my engine running." She is not "on and off"--she is always going. She doesn't have to turn on and off, and she can speed up and slow down naturally. I can't do that. So I have learned to busy myself when she throttles down. On her side, she has learned to find things to keep me occupied.

She lets me sleep till the project is ready to go. Then I'm going as long as it's going. Twelve hours? Fifteen hours? For weeks on end? We've done that together when we had to leave an apartment and prep the glorious living space we are now … including building walls and flooring. She gets me at 100% throughout the day of working on the project, and then when I'm done, I turn the engine off and am basically useless.

What do we "not" do? (This is the big thing.)

We do not expect that we work the same way *and get angry when we're different*. We figure out how each other works and find the best efficient balance to get done what we need to get done. We do this with observation and care.

She does not force my body to do something that makes it works inefficient, and I do my best to be at my most energetically efficient.

I do not clamp down on her when her creative impulses

lead to adjustments in our work schedule.

Respect the nesting, respect the resting. It's about the **respect**.

The other description in the header for this section is "Ladder/Non-Sequitur." This is basically the same idea, but in place for mental energy rather than physical. It is focused on the idea that my mind naturally performs mental actions linearly as the part of a larger system, whereas my mate can think in a fully abstract manner.

This means that each moment I am engaging in thinking I am moving generally from one rung of a ladder to the next. When I am planning my day, I move from one solid idea of what I'm doing to the next in my head, setting them all in a row. If something gets adjusted, I usually have to reset the entire thing. If I am in the middle of doing something and I get interrupted, I can get completely lost. Maybe this is just me, but I have seen it quite a bit with men. When a rung of my ladder gets moved, my ladder generally breaks, and I have to rebuild it. This is what my mind has found to be the most efficient use of my mental energy.

My mate has plans for her day, but they can dissolve and reappear and change with no issues at all. She knows intuitively what is going on in her day without needing to move in an organized fashion from one thing to another. She can Non-Sequitur from what she's doing to something else at any given time, and change plans without even breaking stride. I envy her that ability and I am trying to find ways of doing it.

How does this play out, though? It plays out in this way …

I am cooking beef stroganoff and on my mental step 5,

putting the cauliflower in the pot to be steamed. She comes into the kitchen and decides that she wants the cauliflower done in the microwave because she doesn't want the extra pot. Totally makes sense *and is a great idea*. But now I have no idea what step I'm on and what is supposed to be done next. I've lost step 5. That likely changes the other steps. How do I remember to do step 9 if step 8 is different?

Long story short, I burn the rice. I forgot to set the timer.

Now I could get all resentful and blame her for the idea she had because I know it led to me burning the rice, which I feel guilty about (besides the discomfort of cleaning a burnt pan). On her end, she could be oblivious to the effect her changing things up on me had. But WE DON'T DO THAT. We learn each other.

After years of living together, when she gets engaged in something I'm doing, she asks if her idea is going to mess with me. This takes all of two seconds. On my end, I keep myself as much on my toes as I can be, knowing that I may have to adjust my plans if she has an awesome idea.

What it leads to?

It leads to respect for each other's process and much less loss (a portion of rice is by no means the most that can be lost). We work with each other rather than guilting each other *for being the way we are* when it impedes the way we naturally want to do things. Peace of mind is much easier to keep as the foundation in the household as a direct result.

She knows that my Ladder helps me work efficiently. I respect the pure genius that her non-sequiturs can bring in to any situation. So we work WITH those, even though they are a little foreign to us.

I know that this may seem like a basic idea, but trying to be roommates for 30-40 years is a pretty insane proposition if we don't learn each other and try to work with the quirks and confusing elements of those we love.

Whatever it is about us that creates friction with our partners, we can get better at it. We can focus more on it. Women can try to tone themselves down a little and recognize their mood fluctuations faster. Men can stay present longer when they're uncomfortable. Everyone can communicate more clearly and use breath to consciously release tension rather than letting anger build. Everyone can regard each other's space a little better. And everyone can be patient with their partner while they work on these things.

What we don't want to happen is resentment. Resentment is the death of all things beautiful, and I have found that understanding the nature of women and men better has kept me from feeling slighted when they are "just doing their thing," and helped me remain more patient while they "got better at doing their thing."

Chapter 16:

The Relationship House

I love the Relationship House. When I first put this description together, I got warm all over and stayed that way for the remainder of the day. It was freeing. I had been thinking of relationships as "united" or "adversarial" for so long that I had not even considered that there was a completely separate entity with characteristics and demands that existed. It was freeing to know that the "difficulties" were not being created by the two people involved, but by the reality of "living in union." In that moment, fault and blame and battling seemed to recede into the distance, and honor and accountability jumped forward.

The Relationship House is the symbol of the synergetic union between two people that exists external to them. While this exists in all relationships to "some" extent, in *relationship unions it is the HOME.* It is where trust is fostered or lost, where love is grown or abandoned, where creativity and respect are nurtured or rejected … and based on whether the relationship contains more of the former pairs or the latter, it is the place the *relationship flourishes* … or crumbles to the ground in an awful messy pile of debris.

One of the best parts of falling in love is that it feels like we were given something amazing. And, honestly, we were.

Finding the House

Every time I started a relationship in my life, it felt like I was given something precious. Often, I had worked hard to get it. I was quite the "courter" in my youth and loved watching a beautiful connection appear between myself and someone else.

I have experienced watching others have this happen to them for a long time. I am a huge fan of love and romance, a huge fan of intimacy. As a result, I have studied and integrated the timelines for relationships. The Honeymoon phase, the Nesting phase, the 18-month Oxytocin dip, etc. There are plenty after, plenty in marriage, but I was mostly interested in the phases *before people stopped continuously falling in love*. I never got why people stopped falling in love. What was happening?

With the discovery of the Relationship House, I had a new way to look at all of these stages and figure out what was going on IN THE HOUSE rather than BETWEEN THE TWO PEOPLE. That was a huge distinction.

The truth is that it's not just about the two people. It's about everything they have ever been connected to and the type of structure that their connection called into being. I have found that some structures are stronger than others, regardless of what type of people are actually involved in the union. I tried to figure out why for some time ... then I realized it wasn't important and moved on. What IS important is that we understand what the Relationship House is and prepare ourselves to work with it the best we can.

The difference between what I used to see when people fell in love, and what I see now, can best be described by what I am going to say next. When people fall in love, it's like finding a house. Finding "home." Finding a place where they are welcome and safe. But … it's like *moving into an actual house*. When you find it and move in, it is totally ready and working properly. It is given to you in perfect pristine shape. But like any house, it needs UPKEEP. Every single day we are dirtying and creating wear and tear on every single feature of the house. So, when we first move in, it's the Honeymoon. It's like someone else is cleaning our hotel room and all we have to do is eat and sleep and enjoy each other. After that is the Nesting phase, when we personalize the space with art and share our individual identities with the space we are living in. Then we hit eighteen months … and the house looks like crap because we haven't taken care of it.

Every relationship, after eighteen months, will look like absolute garbage to people who have no idea how to self-manage and take care of a relationship. And since we are not taught about this, it's 99% of people. Think of going on a honeymoon. Think of someone coming in to clean up after you and your love for weeks. Feel that joy. Does it remind you of the honeymoon phase of relationships? Can't you feel it? I can. Now, think of being in a hotel room for a week, but no one has come in to clean. Everything is dirty, and smelly, and instead of intimacy being an amazing joy, it kinda smells funny and is a little too close to living in a zoo.

What I think happens is that the moment we start to notice that the relationship doesn't clean up after itself, that it needs constant tending, we start shoving issues that come up under the bed and into the closet and garage and basement. Eighteen months is when those areas overflow and the bullshit we've been hiding and not dealing with soils the house, making it unlivable. Does the oxytocin supposedly dip then? Yes. Do I think that is because of random pheromone issues? No. I think it's because after not dealing with the up-keep of the relationship the house has broken down and is no longer livable. That's on us, not chemistry.

We think that finding the house is the biggest thing. We make movies about finding the house that exacerbate the problem. The problem is that we don't know anything about upkeep. We glorify falling in love and do not glorify self-dis-covery and working to harmonize with those we love.

What I can tell you to motivate you into this new arena? If you focus on self-discovery and management, you get to fall in love over and over forever.

Let me say that again. If you learn to work with your mate on upkeep, ***you get to fall in love over and over forever***. That means that the best part of being in a relationship is the thing you get to do over and over again … if you put in the work.

"Get all your shit, we're moving in!"

It's exactly like that. We've found this amazing thing, and now we have to bring everything we own in and find a place for it. This is the physical, the mental, the emotional, and the spiritual. Nothing is left behind. All the skills and tools come in with us as well as all the trauma and garbage.

Every single shred of who we are crosses the threshold of the new place, but not all of it stays together in one room. In general, we show off and celebrate our skills and successes, while the rest gets put into storage. Unfortunately … nothing can stay in storage forever.

The Untrained Pets and Their Effect on House Maintenance

Most of Relationship House upkeep is spread across the many chapters of this book, so listing every bit would be redundant. There is a facet of it that I do want to cover, because it has little to do with the house itself; rather, it has to do with the crap we bring in with us. Some elements of our personality are forged by events that scarred us or left us in stages of deep loss and abandonment. This is normal. In order to survive these traumas, our psyche compartmentalized these parts of our being … and in doing so, *gave them extended life.* It gives them life, because when we refuse to engage something, we lose the opportunity to manage it (we can't train an animal we don't believe exists).

When we do not process trauma, we give power to that specific pain. Thus, in the future when it decides it wants to make itself a part of our lives, it will have the ability to do so. Repressing is for short-term survival, yes. But it ends up *creating a long-term relationship with trauma.* Basically, we have gained a pet.

So, rather than describe these aspects of ourselves as "things," like they're cute quirks or something, I'm going to harken back to a description from CFC101 and describe them as wild, unruly animals. I believe this to be wholly more accurate.

The parts of ourselves that we are not so proud of, or have no healthy way of dealing with, get tossed into storage. I consider the storage area for this to be the basement of the

Relationship House (I chose basement over garage or shed, because if they are not dealt with, *they eat the foundation*, not the yard). So, just imagine that you've walked into this beautiful house, and locked a bunch of nasty dirty wild pets in the basement. This is what we ALL do in our relationships. Yes, all. We all have a bag of nasty that gets thrown somewhere to be dealt with later, or more likely, never. The biggest question about this bag is this: "Do we even know what animals are in there? Does the person we're with know what animals are in theirs?"

I'm getting flashbacks to writing the "Know Your Tragedy" chapter.

In order to figure out what pets are in our nasty bag and how to watch out for them, we have to ask ourselves the following question: "**How does what happened to us affect our behavior now**?"

Each untrained animal in our basement is ours to train. Each animal is ours to engage. You may be wondering if I mean "just the ones we brought in" or not. Nope. All animals can damage the house, so all animals need to be engaged. The truth, though, is that the person who brought them in has the best and only real chance to tame and domesticate them, as they are the one who resisted them in the first place. Most of the time we train our own … though I believe there are exceptions.

How do we train them?

1) Know they exist. If you haven't identified all of yours or your partner hasn't, it's a good idea to just *be ready to identify them* when they appear.

2) Watch their behavior, and understand what messes they like to make and what damage they like to do. I can assure

you that my "old heartbreaks and betrayals" behave very differently when they are free roaming than my "fear of doctors" does.

3) Realize that their main power is in the EMOTIONAL ACTIVATIONS they cause within us and the motivated *behavior that arises from that discomfort.*

4) Discuss them with our Divine Other so that both parties can be aware of their presence and on the lookout for their emergence form the basement.

5) When they show up, don't freak out. They will be inappropriate for the situation, confusing, and they will aim to knock you off balance and ASSERT THEIR AUTHORITY by dominating our feelings and behavior.

6) Don't resist their presence, but don't let them dominate. Do not repress … *process.*

7) Know that this practice will *domesticate* them over time, not remove them. Validate the action taken with yourself and your mate if they were involved.

That's how we do it. The feelings come up and get processed, no one gets dominated so behaviors don't get out of hand, and everyone understands what's going on and that it's part of the healing process of living a full life.

When we can handle our own unruly pets, it makes our mates feel safe, and inspires them to move forward with engaging theirs. As we grow in a relationship and get better at this, we begin to look forward to it rather than just trying to survive it.

If we don't engage these pets of ours? They will eat the foundation of the house. They will break into regular moments and emotionally activate us, dominating and influencing our behavior. That behavior will alienate our Divine Other, and activate guilt and shame within us. That's how the ghosts of our past live with us and haunt us in the present. They, if not consciously engaged, turn us into awful versions of ourselves at the most vulnerable times.

The messy stuff within us is a part of us. That is not going to change. How those parts of us affect and influence us is up for negotiation through conscious effort.

Have no doubts that *what we bring into the Relationship House is likely the thing that will destroy the Relationship House*. Have no doubts that even if we are working together in a skilled capacity, it will be a challenge to keep the house together. Have no doubts that if either person is not working to engage these unruly basement-dwellers, the house is likely to fall to ruin.

The Relationship House is the greatest gift I have ever received, and making my House run smoothly is the greatest SKILL I HAVE EVER LEARNED. But, have no doubts that the former does not include the latter, and that the Relationship House's only hope for survival is in inspiring the latter.

Chapter 17:

... CFC Chapter 17 Part 2: Blessings in Expression ... Love

This is the chapter I wrote on love as a blessing in my first book. I am going to edit it for size and any redundant content.

Love, *as a feeling,* is subjectively powerful ... and objectively trivial. If we have the ability to express that feeling healthily, ***it is objectively powerful***. Being able to express it healthily is honoring it, and that is pivotal for our lives. That ability will be the creative force in the construction of whatever beauty exists in our world, will allow us to fall asleep more easily as we grow old, and will find as a foundation for peace on our deathbeds.

Love, as a feeling, is objectively trivial.

Love is not a behavior. Love is something inside of us that needs to be translated into the world through us. That translation is vital. It is the *birthing process* that either brings the love we feel into the world, or twists and perverts it into something unusable, or destructive.

Newborn babies love their mothers. Unadulterated joy washes over them like heroin at the sound or sight of their mother. But they are not capable of translating that love into anything besides big smiles and cuteness. This is not a judgment on their ability to feel love, it is *pointing out a limitation on their ability to show/give love.*

In truth, we are all limited in our ability to show love. How limited we are determines whether we are capable of actively loving anything at all. Many people are so inept at translating love that their innermost feelings are never honored through their actions, and thus their love never manifests in reality.

We have a way in our society of "missing the point" when it comes to the external judgment of love. This is to protect ourselves from self-judgment and cognitive dissonance. It makes sense. When we look at people's behaviors, we judge their feelings. This is because we do not want to confront the fact that we can feel great love for someone and act in a totally unloving manner toward them. *That is not an incongruent reality, and that fact is frightening.*

"How can they love someone and _____" (Insert questionable behavior here).

We pose questions that we assume cannot be answered. How can a person love someone and beat them? How can a person love someone and betray them? How can a person love someone and undermine their health and growth? How can a person feel one way and act in a manner that seems contrary? Easy. **Feelings do not create behaviors.** They can influence them, but they do not create them.

So this is the situation. **A person can love math and fail a math test**. There is no substitute for study and practice. But at least with school subjects, like math, we know what we are studying and that *studying is important*. When it comes to human beings, we do not know how to study, what to study, or even THAT WE NEED TO BE STUDYING. Goodness.

A good description of this idea can be shown with man's best friend. My dog loves me. It is a true thing. His ability to love me is not limited by his feelings. His ability to love me is limited by his physical attributes and by his understanding of the world around him.

If this is a tough one for you to picture, take your picture of a loving dog, and give him thumbs and increase his intelligence tenfold. Give him the ability to read. Now think of how much more awesome the world around him is. Think of all the extra chores that get done around the house. Think of the amount of care this pooch would put into everything and how tirelessly he would work to keep in the light of your affection. The dog that killed and dragged a raccoon onto your porch *would totally do the dishes forever*.

So why do we dance around the idea of feeling love as if it were this holy thing that determined the quality of behaviors?

The first reason is because we do not want to face the consequences of realizing that our deepest feelings are inconsequential when it comes to our behavior. We want to be able to say "I love them so much that I am going to _____" (insert truly insane idea here), and *have our **feeling** be the justification* for the action. Stalking is the obvious one that comes to mind.

The second reason we do not want to face this is because *it means we are never done working*. We always have to keep learning about the world and the people we care about. The pressure of keeping up with this is so daunting that we'd rather just pretend it wasn't true.

I don't blame anyone for wanting this truth to go away. Heck, I want it to go away. In fact, here's an example of my self-diagnosis for what I desired when I was younger ....

What do I really want?

"I want the feeling of love that I carry within me to create the exact right behavior in every situation. I want this to be instinctual and last forever. I also do not want the possibility of error, because the feeling I have has no error in it, so neither should the behavior that it generates. I also do not want it to ever come into conflict with any other feelings in myself or others. THAT IS WHAT I WANT. I do not want to have to *negotiate* this want. And I want it so badly that I am willing to pretend it is true."

To this day I have to struggle to honor my love for things through the process of living and learning.

Live and learn. We get better at most everything as we get older. Learning how to love people is a really taxing job. It is frustrating. It is frustrating because we are continually learning more about the nature of health, the nature of our environment, and the nature of the world around us. It is even more frustrating because the living objects of our love are constantly changing in every possible way.

We are truly ill-equipped to manage this situation. Even those of us who deeply devote ourselves to our favorite human beings and have extensive knowledge of health, psychology, nutrition, are, more often than not, totally lost.

Here is another situation where *having an accurate picture of the inherent difficulty of a task gives us direction*. The perspective matters. Seeing ourselves as naturals in translating the feeling of love into an expression *cripples us*. It cripples us because we take it personally when our efforts are failures. It cripples us because we do not know that a constant state of evolving is necessary to honor the love we feel. We cannot prepare if we truly believe we are already masters. **Knowing we are never ready is a priceless motivation**. It makes us ask questions, and makes us patient observers while awaiting answers.

So, say it with me: "*The love I feel is perfect. It is glorious and divine. My ability to honor that love through action is limited by my knowledge and focus. My great feeling of love deserves my unending effort.*"

Asking the Right Questions ... Prepping to Teach Classes

How does love manifest? Let's say someone loves music; what questions do we have about them given that fact?

What type of music do they like? How many albums do they own? Have they studied music? Can they play music? Which musicians are their favorites? How do they use music to make their lives better? How often do they engage with music, by playing or listening?

We have some expectations here. If someone says they love movies or art, we have expectations there as well. We expect that certain behaviors have been born of the feelings someone declares they have. We expect that they are engaging the object of their love.

But when someone says they love someone, which is a huge, life-changing reality in someone's world … we rarely ask the right questions.

"Oh, you love your husband? So you've studied psychology and nutrition, right? What's his blood type? How does his history motivate him on a daily basis? How is his body aging? How has he changed recently? How does he scare you? How does he make you feel more alive? What are you looking forward for him as far as his emotional growth goes? What projects make him feel alive, and how are you helping him to achieve his goals in those areas? In what ways do you strengthen yourself as to add to the health of his environment?"

Ever heard those questions asked before?

If I love someone, I want to be able to answer EVERY question above in detail. In fact, what I want is exact. I want to be able to teach an entire class on everyone I love. Now it may be true that I can give only a two-hour lecture on my grandfather, but I'd better be able to give you a full semester on my mate and kids.

It might seem like I'm asking too much, **but it is not me that is asking it**. Love asks to be honored. It asks to be manifest in reality. The feelings we have demand an avenue for expression. My love demands it. So does yours. And for the glory of life that love bestows upon us, this is not asking much.

So how do we prepare ourselves to teach a class on a human being?

There are really only three big things to focus on. First, it is vitally important that we learn the mechanisms that all human beings share. We all have bodies. We all have minds. We all have histories and genetics and experiences that shape our perspectives and inner realities. The way that all of these things affect us can vary slightly from person to person, as all of those have variables built into them. The understanding of the human body, mind, and experiences that form the matrix of life are the core concepts, learning those *strengthens our ability to learn* the people we love. No matter where we apply this knowledge, it is helpful. It is never a waste of time or energy (especially since we are one of the people we apply it to). This includes zeroing in on specific traits within medicine and psychology that our loved ones present to us. Do they have allergies? What is their astrological sign? What is their ethnicity? What can we learn about them by the subsets of groups they are included in?

The second part is paying attention to something we love. It's pretty simple, but it does demand that we focus even when we are distracted and that we care enough to find the changes that occur. That gets difficult and is demanding. As fathers and mothers, we may not want to see our children growing up. As husbands and wives, we do not want to see love fading, or attention fixing in other areas. This is normal. We fear change. Hopefully we get used to it before it stops us from being able to see changes in the ones we love that are closest to us. Hopefully.

The third is keeping ourselves in good, conscious shape. We are not capable of learning anything about anyone if we are not operating from a healthy focus. We are not capable of observing clearly and openly. If we are operating from fearful perspectives, or are worn down by stress or illness, we are not going to be able to keep up with the subject matter. We will not be able to keep up, because we will not be "present."

"Some blessings come with prerequisites." – Steven Jackson, NFL Running back.

We want to have the ability to love in a way that honors our feelings. But my description of love is in a chapter with the title of "blessings of expression," because there are prerequisites that must be met before we are capable of really *engaging in loving behavior* and focus.

I mentioned previously that when learning someone we had to be in good mental and emotional shape. This is true. If we are not in good shape we cannot be present. *We cannot actively love anyone if we are not present.* If we are present, we can express love, anger, joy, violence, and anything we feel within us. If we are not present, we can only express absence.

Learning and understanding someone makes us feel safe. That makes us capable of creating space for more love. When I mentioned that we cannot express love when we are not present, it means that whatever makes us stressed, frightened, and angry is capable of denying our heart its outlet through our being. Since there are major issues we all face (like rejection, confusion, and shock), it is easy for us to be much closer to fear, rather than a place of safety when it comes to those closest to us. The truth is that this fear is *totally justified*, because the people we love and are vulnerable with will always have the greatest ability to hurt us. Learning others can ease the distress we feel that is caused by this fact. I want to show some ways that learning our loved ones can ease our levels of stress and fear and allow us to more fully engage them.

How do we ease stress and fear for the purpose of heightened engagement?

I know a lot about the people I love. This allows me an opportunity that I consider a great blessing. It allows me *the ability to love bountifully*.

There are things I know about everyone in my world that help me live harmoniously with them. In the following examples, I am going to show how I, and people I know closely, use knowledge to relieve stress, feel safe, and give love. I will present those along with descriptions of what NOT having that information could look like. When I mention what not having the knowledge entails, it may look like I'm being dramatic ... but while subtle ways we improve our world may seem tedious and trivial at times, they are crucially important.

Situation 1.

My nephew has issues with gluten and sugar. He gets beyond cranky. He gets out of control and violent if his chemistry is not in balance.

The knowledge we have: My sister in law knows how gluten and sugar work with the body. Over time she has become very attentive to even the most minor changes in his physiology throughout the day. She pays attention to him, and thus can watch the fluctuations of his mood with enough focus to feed him what he needs, when he needs it.

The result: My nephew is an awesome, well-behaved kid. He trusts the people around him and the world to meet is needs. He is less prone to acting out. When he gets close to having a meltdown, my sister in law can react with the proper food and attention to make it less painful for him. That's the primary result.

The secondary result is for my sis in-law. Instead of being confused and frightened all the time about my nephew's mood swings, she can relax and just provide him with what he needs when he needs it. This makes the entire household run more smoothly.

The result for a family that had not found out about the gluten issues: The violence would not have abated at a young age and the acting out would have gotten worse. The family would all be tense, as there are four children, and my sis-in-law and brother would be in a constant state of worry over my nephew's erratic moods and destructive behavior. It is unlikely that he would be able to attend school. and the strain on the family as a whole would be gigantic, removing the likelihood that the other children get their needs met. It would be very difficult for anyone to visit, or extremely stressful if they did.

That was just *understanding a gluten sensitivity*. But how many of us do the necessary research to help those we love? Many of us try, and either cannot find the correct answers, or do not have access to the right resources when we do find the correct answers. If we do find the right information, it still takes tireless effort and focus. *The whole of that endeavor, is an expression of love.*

(I am four years removed from having written this as I put it into this book … and can add that my nephew is an amazing young man.)

Situation 2.

My oldest is twelve. That, in itself, is an issue. Puberty is an insane time for boys and girls, where their actions are bigger and bear more consequence, at a time when they have the least amount of control over their actions and impulses. My oldest is loud, prone to wild mood swings, violent with his brother, forgetful of important things, and over-reactive. Puberty is like being on drugs.

The knowledge we have: I know that his mind is expanding and hungry. I know that he is hugely frustrated by everything everywhere and has no idea how to control or even relate to his ever-changing emotional matrix. I know that his levels of stress directly relate to how he will grow emotionally during this period. I know that our responses as parents can give him stability and boundaries, which he needs during this process. I also know that my reactions need to be really tempered by my understanding of where he is. It is normal that he feels uncomfortable, because that means he is imprinting new concepts that he will use the rest of his life.

The result: We get a young man who is capable of asking for time alone. We get a young man who makes mistakes, and has consequences, but does not live in fear. His ease and comfort make him capable of allowing himself to go through frustrating cycles, learning to process emotions without reining in his nature due to fear of what those expressions will cause. He feels understood and listened to. He does not feel alone because we can mirror back to him what he is feeling and validate his growth. And due to all of those factors, this growth period is not violent or alienating for him.

The result for a family that does not know about adolescent psychology: The child becomes increasingly frightened and stressed because his mood fluctuations are taken very seriously, and he becomes afraid to express himself. He begins to withdraw and act out. He seeks help, seeks feeling understood and safe, but finds a frustrated parenting unit perplexed by his irrational and ever-changing behavior. He lives scared. He does not act on his instincts, and begins to mistrust himself. He begins to feel alone. Thus, he begins to keep his internal reality under lock and key. He and his parents lose touch. He has the choice of disappearing completely within himself or finding ways to ask for help. These ways get more attention the more destructive they are. The child spends years trying to understand himself, searching to feel known and loved by those around him. He becomes resentful and disengaged.

This is just puberty. While people and expressions vary, we can all do more to treat this time period as *the crazed author of the future adult* that it is. Patience and calm reactions to the many changes within the previously stable mind of a child are essential for their development.

(Four years later … my oldest is the most emotionally intelligent person I could imagine any fifteen-year-old being.)

Situation 3.

My mate is a Gemini. I was not a huge fan of astrology. I could have taken my skepticism and walked with it, but I would ignoring a possible tool if I did, and I knew it. So … I became familiar with what it means to share my life with a Gemini.

The knowledge that understanding a Gemini affords me: I know that she can hold two opposing viewpoints and experience untold amounts of stress as a result. She can draw from these opposing viewpoints at any moment and switch back and forth. She can want a combination of things that are incompatible. That is normal for a Gemini. For me, her focus looks like steering two cars at once and randomly choosing which roadway she is reacting to. That is what it looks like to me, *but that is NOT what she sees*. She'll be steering on a mountain road in one perspective and on a drag strip in the other and I don't know what's going to happen when she gets to a turn. All judgments about this aside, this is scary for me. I cannot believe that it works, because I CAN'T WORK IT. But it's not my business to make it work, it's my business *to let her work it*. That is where my responsibility can end. I don't have to be stressed out. The only way she can find out which landscape she wants is by steering in both until she is moved to pick one. Until then I treat both as real, because they are, even if to me they look incompatible. She is expertly working schemata that I have no ability to even conceptualize.

The result of my knowledge: I can watch her bounce around within the same perspective in ways I cannot wrap my mind around. I can relax. And when I'm relaxed, she'll find out what she wants faster, and with less stress.

The result of NOT having that knowledge: I get nervous. It makes her nervous. I get into cycles of fear each time she is making a decision. She begins to feel guilty about the way she thinks and makes decisions. She starts to hide it from me, or feel nervous tension every time it occurs. Worst-case scenario is that she feels so uncomfortable she becomes resentful and leaves the relationship.

(She's still a Gemini, and I still don't get it. But I have better theories now on why astrology is impactful.)

These are all examples of perspectives we undertake to make life more awesome for the people around us. We undertake these perspectives out of respect for their experience. Respect lies in the non-dismissal of whatever their reality entails. If their realities lie outside of our sphere of understanding and control, *we work outside of our comfort zone*, rather than dismissing part them to make them fit into a container we understand.

We live a life filled with sound-bites of people "not getting" this. "Why can't she just be happy?" "Why can't he stop drinking?" "Why can't they get over it?" "Why can't they control it?" "Why don't they understand?" "Why doesn't he let his emotions out?" "Why does it always have to be a fight?" "Why doesn't she make up her damn mind?" "Oh my God they make me so crazy!"

Those are all the same question: "WHY DOESN'T THIS PERSON FIT INTO MY PICTURE OF WHAT REALITY SHOULD BE LIKE FOR THEM." Yeah. It's not their problem, *it's ours*. If we want to see ourselves as loving another person, it's best to get those questions and translate them into what they are. **They are ALL a call to action**. They are the call to UNDERSTAND THE PERSON WE LOVE MORE FULLY.

We do not have to become part of a cycle of rejection with them. We do not have to get freaked out and reject their situation ... then have them feel rejected and pull away. Knowledge about the ones we love makes us unlikely to be frightened and defensive about their way of relating to the world around them. Each human being is an entire culture, with a language, a science, and a history. Being a good student is a vital prerequisite for learning how to love.

Study and focus into areas of our loved ones' lives will yield results that are pivotal to the survival of any relationship. Understanding the internal realities and motivations of people we love creates a *LARGER SHARED REALITY* between us. That brings us to the final and most important aspect of loving. Knowing, understanding, and loving ... the self.

This is not the proverbial "know thyself" of philosophical ambiguity ... this is a "know thyself" that relates to how we are capable of loving ourselves or something/someone else. It ends up being nearly the same course material, but with a different applied focus. The focus is different, because *we* are teaching the class on *ourselves* to *someone else*. How well can we teach THAT class to another person as it relates to our relationship with them?

This is not "How well do you know yourself?" ... this is "How well can you explain yourself to each unique person in your life?" It is not just about sharing our hearts and minds with those we love. It is about protecting others.

For anyone we are close to, we have the ability to hurt them intimately and deeply. They are the audience that will get any excess violence that we need to express. They will be the beneficiaries of any unmanaged aggression.

We also need to focus on teaching others how to understand our language. Misunderstandings are powerful and all too common, as is our ability to take everything personally. None of that is helpful.

The more we know about ourselves and can share with others, the more likely we are to be able to skirt around the many landmines that can present themselves in everyday situations. The more comfortable we get with maneuvering these hazards in concert with another person, the more of ourselves we can safely share. That means more of our pain can be healed and more of our joy expanded.

Knowing the Vito and Teaching the Vito. Protection and Enrichment.

I have been pretty good my whole life about not making myself more complex than I have to be. It's very rare that I force people to figure things out and there is not much that lies beneath the surface.

I have PTSD. I am bipolar. I have six years of college under my belt, and twenty years of organized study that I carry around with me. I love football. I have been an addict and a drunk. I have been an adrenaline junkie. I was a musician and I care a ton about music. I am very tuned to visual intuition. I am an ambivert (super social one minute, an introvert the next). I can have debilitating panic attacks that can be brought on by *anything*. I need seven hours of sleep uninterrupted or I am not going to be myself. I take meds, and I need them in order to operate normally. I am compulsive. I frustrate easily.

That is what Vito looks like on paper for the most part. *That is the outline of the class I am going to teach on myself.*

The class changes for every person I am teaching. That is my job. My job as a Vito, and your job as a you, is to adjust the class to the **Audience** we are addressing. The content changes, the length of the class changes, and my language changes. My mate, my children, my coworkers, my friends, my clients … they all get different voices tailored to their learning styles and content appropriate for the growth of *that* relationship. Explaining ourselves is not just about us and what we want to express about ourselves. It is about everyone, *because growth is about everyone.*

It is more difficult than I have stated here. It seems like "finding the right voice" to speak with someone shouldn't be that hard. But it is. It is especially hard with sensitive issues, if we fear rejection, or we are in danger. On top of all that, it is difficult if we are asking for help. Those moments are the ones that demand clarity of communication the most, *and they are the most difficult to navigate successfully.*

Now what does this have to do with love and prerequisites? I can tell you that if I had never gotten my description of myself across correctly to my tenth psychologist (yes, tenth, it took me that long to adequately explain myself to a professional), I would not be where I am. Not close. I would still have been dealing with the issue of mental instability. I was not capable of safely loving anyone, or even *protecting others from my instability.* I needed help. And in order to get help, I had to be able to communicate with someone that could help me.

The difficulty is obvious with psychologists, as they are strangers and have to build an entire profile of my life based on what I tell them. But the difficulty is everywhere and it is imperative that we do not get too frustrated, because we cannot ever give up on communicating our experience. My mother had to live with me through some rough years. I was drinking heavily (basically all day long) and having panic attacks daily.

I remember that I had tried to explain the feelings that led to drinking on a daily basis for five years. We had to have talked about it a hundred times. She said she understood my description, but then she would ask questions that led me to believe she did not. *So I did not give up.* After five years, I found an analogy that described the combination of a panic attack, energy overload, and its physical component, in the necessary manner to get my point across.

Not only did that breakthrough give me peace and satisfaction (which was a huge weight lifted), it provided her and me both with means of protecting each other. Her focus had always been to try to help me *control a panic attack*. That is not only impossible, but painful. When someone is trying to "reason" you out of a panic attack, it is insulting, frustrating, and infuriating … and they do not mean it to be. When I finally got myself across fully, *she stopped accidentally hurting me*. When I am in a bad panic attack, I am in awful *physical pain*. But the pain is REALLY difficult to express in words. She would tell me that I was safe, and show me that my surroundings were secure. She did that because she could not understand how the pain was affecting me (as I actually was not safe). The fact that she couldn't understand the pain made me feel even less safe. It made me angry. It frustrated me. It hurt my feelings. *And all of those things together made the panic worse.*

I was like a grease fire. She could only use her tools and knowledge of my situation. Until I broke through the gap in our communication she would simply see that I was on fire, and douse me with water. But I was a grease fire. So every day she made it worse by accident, because I could only say "I'm on fire!!!" really loud. At this point she would toss water on me, making the fire worse. I was doing my best, and she was doing her best. **It wasn't good enough**.

That is a frustrating thing, beyond what I could ever explain. It doesn't seem like it should be that hard, or that it could be that hard. But it is. She was my mother, a therapist, and we had lived together for twenty years of my life. AND IT STILL TOOK ME FIVE YEARS TO EXPLAIN. That was humbling.

We can see how teaching the class on Vito is going to be different in every exercise. It is also never to be underestimated. It's important that I know it backwards and forwards. My bipolar disorder and PTSD, panic attacks, etc. ... they have been a part of my life for a long time. I consider myself lucky to have been gifted with some extra challenges in the area of consciousness, because it has afforded me the necessary "forced attention" that led to everything I write about.

Learning the manner in which I can best explain myself to others has been irreplaceable for my relationship with my mate. I have spoken about how I teach myself to strangers, and how I teach myself to family. This is how I go about continuing to teach in my **Primary Relationship** (I am calling this the "Divine Other" in this book).

The issue with our Primary Relationship that gets us into trouble, and why I believe getting engaged with teaching a class in ourselves is so difficult, is that we have to be vulnerable to someone we want to see us as powerful.

"Are you okay?" I have heard that question a million times from my mate and my boys. They know that being around other people in public places can rile me up and get me flustered. They also know that if it gets bad I will be a wreck for an entire day. That is no fun for anyone and can severely alter our plans. Over time, being able to use that question to protect things from getting out of hand has enabled me to do things I never could have done otherwise. When my mate, or my boys ask me if I'm okay ... when I answer, **I have to be right**. I cannot love them if I am not stable, and we cannot work together to keep me from becoming unstable *unless they know exactly where I am*. This means that I must have constant, clear observation of where my emotions are and be able to give an immediate account.

Answers to this question range from "happy and mellow" to "totally messed up." I have been asked this question while driving us home, and upon my answer "Umm, I don't know exactly how I am," we stopped the car and my mate took the wheel so I could mellow out in the passenger seat. Sometimes she asks while I'm driving and I say, "Not so good, but the driving is helping me and I'm focused and safe."

If I am not safe, or am not sure if I am safe to drive, I tell her. **That is really embarrassing**. It's really not fun for me to admit that I have, for no apparent reason, lost the level of consciousness I require to drive a car safely. But I love her, and not telling her is putting her at risk. *That is unacceptable.*

In order for me to put those I love in the best position possible for joy and health, I have to know where I am and what it means for them. I can tell my kids I'm not doing well, am angry or panicked, and that *validates what they saw* that made them ask the question. Then I know enough to absolve them of guilt, blame, and responsibility. That is how I protect them.

I can tell my mate that I am about to lose it, or have gotten flustered by something or someone, *and trust that she will not resent me, use it against me*, or ruin her day trying to help me. She will ask me what level of attention I need for help, and I almost always know how much it is. *"I've got this one," "I want to try to get this one, but I may miss," "Need help when you get a second,"* and *"Need you right now,"* are statements that determine actions in my household and are taken seriously.

She wouldn't be able to help if I didn't know where I was. And if she can't help me, then I will spiral down and out and have a "lost day." That means she has a lost day and our boys have a lost day. No fun.

I know myself, and my moods, and my world, and thus can protect those I love from anything about myself that I may not be able to control. My life would not work if I could not do that effectively.

The rough part of explaining this is that the average person without PTSD and anxiety disorders *has no idea that this applies to them too*. We all get weirded out and scared. We all can overreact. Everyone can get crushed by stress or confusion or anger.

My panic attacks keep me from doing normal things, but others' frustrations make them yell and scream at people they love, drink until they have fully escaped consciousness, and unleash loads of transferred rage onto everyone close to them. **We do these things because we do not know ourselves well enough to figure out how to decompress and heal ourselves throughout the day, as well as because we refrain from asking for, and receiving help from those around us.** So, who pays? Our loved ones do.

My panic attacks are a gift to me. Because of them, I learned to manage my entire consciousness. I made friends with the forces that motivate my behavior. Everyone can do that.

Everyone can take their relationship with their reactions and emotions seriously and engage the things about themselves that are volatile, frightened, defensive, or aggressive. Then we can work in concert with those who love us to slowly alleviate their influence.

Telling the person we love (and want always to impress) where we are weak and what we are scared of is epically difficult. While it is risky and often leads to embarrassment, we have to do our best to know our weaknesses and *allow ourselves to be known*. We will not be happy if we do not. We will not feel safe if we do not. We will not be able to express ourselves if we do not. ***I cannot be loved if all of "me" does not present itself***. I cannot be loved unless I show up, and teach those I love to see me.

The power that flows from allowing this risk, and the influence it has over the health, is priceless.

You cannot teach a class on yourself without self-love. That is a love for yourself *that is larger than what you dislike about yourself*. This means that if you pile up all of the things about yourself that make you cringe, and confront yourself with them … you will still like what you see overall and be at peace. That is the threshold. It is not an easy business to succeed in. But anything we do not love about ourselves is not going to get hidden behind us as we step closer to another. It is going to be between us, preventing us from loving fully. Always. That's not where we want it.

The Result of not looking with self-love: Inability to share love. Why self-love is a prerequisite.

The main idea to justify why self-love is a key piece to being able to love another person has to do with equality. However we speak about equality as a society or when discussing politics simply doesn't matter. It is *theory*. Theory is cute and all, and it is where we present ideas that we like, but it has little to do with our motivational-behavior matrix.

The truth is that we know exactly what we are scared of, and how much of ourselves we are able to present to the world around us. We know that we are hiding things. When we do this, *we are making interpersonal equality impossible*.

Everything is always expressing itself. So how does not having self-love express itself by making equality impossible?

1. **We don't look at ourselves**. If we are not too fond of ourselves, we will simply *not look into areas we are uncomfortable with*, and as a result we will not learn. When we do not learn about ourselves, we cannot protect others or get help from others.

   This means *we know we have not looked, and will not feel equal to someone who we believe has*. If we believe they have not looked, then that doesn't make them equal, just puts a different amount of imagination into the inequality.

2. **We feel like a liar**. We know we are not being completely truthful. We know that the person who loves us *loves who they think we are*, not who we *actually are*. Even if, by some chance, they do know us fully without our telling them, *we can never believe that* and have robbed ourselves of the opportunity to trust.

3. **We disable the person who loves us**. "Wow, that person is *dumb* to love me, they don't know how awful I am." "Wow, if that person loves me even though they know I am awful, what a *sucker*." "Wow that person loves me, they must be totally *blind* to all my awful qualities." ***When we cannot love ourselves, WE HAVE TO INVENT A DISABILITY FOR SOMEONE WHO DOES.***

4. **We resent the person who loves us**. "Why do they have to see me so incorrectly? I think I am awful, *why do they*

have to make me feel bad by loving me when I am so un-lovable? Do they think they are better than me? Are they pitying me? Who the hell do they think they are to take pity on me? It makes me so angry that I love someone who is too disabled to see what a scum I am."

5. **We become the swine**. "Do not cast your pearls to swine, lest they trample them underfoot, and *turn on you.*"

   If we are not presenting ourselves fully, or we are be-reft of self-love in the face of someone actually loving us, we will turn on them. This is where "pushing people away" happens. *"I am awful, and you are stupid that you don't know or don't care, so now I'm going to really show you how awful I am, so that I can see the look of fear and disgust on your face* **that echoes how I feel about myself***."*

   How many times in a relationship have we gone way overboard and screamed "Now you can see what I'm *REALLY* like." What's even worse is when the other person does not validate us by looking back at us with the same eyes we use when we look inward at the self we have not fully accepted.

6. **We run**. *If someone can accept us, when we do not, the shame is overwhelming.* If we happen to have the strength to not "turn" on those who love us, we will run until our legs fall off and our entire world burns.

These "reactions" still happen sometimes when we do have self-love. Minor versions of these scenarios play out dur-ing even the best relationships with the healthiest people, be-cause we do not love some "aspects" of ourselves. But it does not get out of hand, *because we love ourselves more than we dislike whatever has come up.* So no matter how overwhelming something we have to deal with feels, our reaction to it will not drive us from engaging and asking for help.

That's the problem with not giving 100 percent of ourselves or hiding the things that we don't like. We are incapable of feeling "deserving." If we do not feel deserving, *we will violently repel anything beyond what little love we believe we deserve*, because we are actually defending ourselves from it. It is too painful to bear the shame of being loved when we do not have self-love, and we will defend ourselves against it.

Love is shared. Self-love allows loving action to flow unhindered. While this is obvious with interpersonal relationships, it is not as obvious when we look at our relationship to society and the world around us.

In the same way we would push another away when they get to close to areas of our realities that make us uncomfortable, we will also push the world away. We will push joy and abundance away. *We will defend ourselves from everything we do not believe we deserve.* We will aggressively and pre-emptively be violent to the world around us.

However, if we achieve the prerequisites for being able to love, then we can be blessed by it. We are blessed with an ability to participate in the world with those we love and honor the feelings we have for them. We are blessed with the ability to present ourselves and be known, to share closeness. We are blessed with knowing that we are expressing that which we believe to be most dear to our heart, in a way that others can rightfully see. We are blessed standing in the Sunlight of our own glory.

And beyond those truths, *we become the blessing* we are capable of being for our loves, ourselves, our reality, and the world. That ability to love becomes a motivational influence on the world itself. This is because love … all love … is shared.

Chapter 18:

Processing Emotion

In all the world, I cannot think of a more important skill to learn or issue to engage than Processing Emotion. I realized, after I finished my first book (CFC101), that the entire text was getting at something from a million different angles. It was getting at the "how to" of Processing Emotion. The inability to process emotion surfaces from many different encounters with the chaotic world we live in, and it cripples the conscious mind. This leaves what should be a sovereign individual ... a resistant, stressed-out, reactive mess.

It is likely that my next book will be focused solely on Processing Emotion. But for now, let's see how this priceless skill can help us when it comes to relating to the world around and inside of us.

If you skipped forward to this chapter, you may want to drop back to Chapter 13 and check the section on Processing Emotion within that chapter so that you have an understanding of what it entails.

Processing Emotion has to be engaged in a relationship *by both individuals* for it to be a dynamic and heart-centered relationship. This is because of a few basic facts of life ...

The Absence of Pain and Frustration DOES NOT EQUAL HAPPINESS

This ends up being a trickier truth than a simple sentence can describe. Clearing frustrations is kind of a job, and dealing with pain is something we generally want to avoid. Both, however, are necessary in order for us to have joy. Feelings all come in through the same door.

The easy thing to tell ourselves is that "the absence of frustration and pain will lead to happiness." It looks true when we see our joy *alongside things that are distracting us* from being able to RELAX. It looks like the frustrations are the most important impediments to joy. If we're not careful, we can trick ourselves into believing that. Joy, in truth, *is separate from*, **yet connected to**, pain and frustration.

The *danger* of believing that pain and joy **are not** connected lies in the fact that we can teach ourselves to resist feelings in general, over time. Our Egoic Mind, if it is persuasive enough, can convince us to learn to shut feelings out completely. Why would it do this? The Egoic Mind does not give a flying flip about happiness … it just wants safety and the illusion of control. We cannot have safety and control when deeply connected to life. This is even truer when dealing with the chaos of a relationship.

In order to keep the **Feelings Door** open, we have to learn to Process Emotion *as a life skill* so that we are not in a constant state of resistance. Can't have a relationship we can't feel.

So how does this work when it is at its most optimal?

Optimally, we allow a huge wall of feelings to stroll right in the front door of our experience; *then we work with them*.

In the art of Conscious Validation, a big tool for the conscious mind I've talked about in this book already, we look to *validate, adjust, or dismiss* thoughts. When it comes to emotion, it is basically the same maneuver, but with more attentive energy and time allotted. This is because where thoughts can be dismissed without issue, feelings need to tell us a story first. Why? No idea. My guess would be that they are not just a vibrational reality, but also that they have a time component within their vibration that *gives them a life span* (that or they need a specific amount of time to pass through body tissues ... both sound reasonable). They are literal "messengers" in this way. This means we have to "sit with" emotions. This is tedious and uncomfortable AT FIRST. It gets easier *over time*. The good news with this is that if we are allowing pain and frustration access to our conscious mind so that they can be processed, joyous states *should be* plentiful as well. These, like helpful thoughts in Conscious Validation, get VALIDATED. In order to validate joy, we "sit with" it as well. That is ACTIVE enjoyment. Consciously allowing ourselves to feel joy is a gracious way of living that activates all the happy and healthy neurotransmitters in the mind, as well activating the immune system.

Optimally, all the feelings come in, *and they get dealt with accordingly*. Optimally, over time, the tedious and uncomfortable aspects become easier to deal with and the joyous aspects become highlighted and accentuated. That's how it works ... **optimally**.

In common practice, it is a focus that reminds us to *allow ourselves a decent amount of discomfort* so that we can stay *as present as possible* for the natural processes of those closest to us. It steers us toward the largest amount of presence so that we can stay connected to our own processes and connected to the processes of the people closest to us. Being focused on allowing discomfort also helps us keep our hearts open in a chaotic and brutal world. This helps us stay connected to the evolution of the human race.

This is how we create and sustain Resonance.

Keeping our doors open to emotion is a winning proposition. If we keep our doors open, we have an opportunity to process the garbage and experience *a greater depth of joy*. If we don't keep the doors open, it does not mean that we are unaffected by the garbage in our lives … **it just means that we can't feel it**. It is STILL with us regardless of whether we feel it, and it gets all over everyone near us.

This is a big deal when it comes to Anger Transference and "being decent roommates" … but it's the biggest deal in the world when it comes to *intimacy*.

Processing Emotion is Sexy

There is a tactile reason that processing emotion is necessary. Arousal. Our intimate depth and our ability to connect with those we love *does not exist separately from our emotional realities*. Our emotions stay with us at all times. What we haven't dealt with during the day, during our lives, between each other … it gets dragged *into the bedroom* with us.

There are terms like "Anger Banging" and "Hate Fucking" that seem to glorify acts of emotional bloodletting through sexual engagement. This is not what I'm talking about in this section. Those are singular moments and generally the processing of the emotion is the focus of the intercourse (or at least a byproduct of it). What I am talking about is unprocessed garbage. This can be frustration and dissatisfaction, but its best example is resentment. Resentment leads to a wholly unsatisfying and disconnected sexual experience. Over time, it leads to sexual experiences where one (or often both parties) would rather be someplace else with someone else. That's not sexy. It is the opposite of sexy.

But … what *is* sexy? Managing guilt, shame, anger, frustration, and despair is sexy. Why? Because instead of going to bed to bed with someone while wearing a mask over all the emotions we want to hide so the person we're with isn't grossed out, we can go to bed and **fully wrap ourselves up in the person we are with**. What a novel concept.

How can we fully touch, love, hug, or make love to someone we are hiding from? Seriously? I have done it plenty in my life, and it was deeply unsatisfying. After a few years I lost my sex drive. I just wasn't interested anymore. Why should I be? Why would anyone be?

I found that the issues I had with myself emotionally … I kept them covered up. I kept them covered in the same way women keep stretch marks or anything they find unsightly about themselves covered up. I figured that since the thing I was covering up was invisible, it would not actually make a difference in the same way that leaving a shirt on during sex because I was ashamed of my scars would. But it did. I believe this to be a consistent human struggle … men and women both affected. To make the point more viscerally, my name for it is the "Soul Condom." It keeps us from being able to really feel anything, regardless of how "safe" we tell our-selves it is. Oddly it reminds me of a line spoken by Owen Wilson in *Wedding Crashers* when asked if he was "totally full of shit or only halfway"… he said, "I hope only half," in a defeated tone.

It didn't matter when I was younger. When I was younger, there wasn't much in my emotional vault that I was ashamed of. As I aged, that vault got bigger. Also, just having sex be-came "not enough." I wanted *deep connection and an attrac-tion that was self-fueling through intimacy*. I wanted to be as satisfied afterwards as I was HUNGRY beforehand.

The amount of emotional debris got more difficult to man-age and I got pickier about what I wanted my experience to be. That's what growing up is. I think this happens for every-one, and I don't know too many people that talk about it.

I have to get into the sack not just with another person, but with all the messed-up things I don't like about myself and the emotions I can't process. That means I am wearing my guilt and shame and fear … and trying to get aroused. Not. Gonna. Happen. Can I make it happen once or twice? Sure. But I'm not gonna be able to keep it up (pun intended).

If we learn to process, and take the time and energy need-ed to do so, we end up feeling raw and vulnerable more often. As a result, we get **more opportunities to connect** with our partners. As a result, those connections not only get deeper, but *the movement into deeper connection becomes a part of the relationship*. That is a priceless reality to move into, espe-cially when both are conscious of it.

It's also hot. It keeps the connection fresh, authentic, dy-namic, and as a result … exciting. It's sexy.

A friend of mine told me an awful story of something her father said to her fiancé at a young age. He said, "Think of your favorite meal. Think of how much you like it. Now think of having to eat that same meal every day for the rest of your life. Are you sure you still want it?" My friend's father was thinking about his own dead sex life and that the only way for him to get excited was to move on to other people. He saw the women he was with as ONE MEAL. That was his *epic* misfortune. And honestly, it was also his fault.

Every single person is a buffet. No person is just a meal. If a person's sexuality is just a meal, it's because we have not gotten close enough to them to witness the many changes they go through on a daily basis. Every emotion and reality we undertake changes our specific flavor, makes us NEW. **This is why sexual attraction in a healthy relationship doesn't fade**. It's why sex doesn't get boring. Because each time the couple engages they are meeting as two totally new people … two totally new people with familiarity who TRUST each other.

Sounds pretty amazing, huh? It is.

It's definitely worth it just for the high-quality sexual aspect. But, it's also necessary to keep the Relationship House in order. Why is it necessary?

Because this world is definitely going to mess with us. It's not a maybe; it's a guaranteed thing.

3D is Non-negotiable

No matter how in love you are, someone has to do the damn laundry. And the dishes. And mow the lawn. And vacuum. That's the basic stuff. Frustrating as hell, but basic.

No matter how in love you are, or how amazing you are at parenting, someone or something is going to mess with your kid. That's infuriating.

No matter how talented and hard-working you both are, someone is going to mess with you or your partner at work. Then there's the grocery store and the mall.

No matter how badass we are, someone is going to mess with us. It's going to happen. It's life.

The question is, **what do these conflicts lead to**? They all lead to frustration and emotional activation, at the very least. That leads to having some "waste energy" to process. I call it "waste energy" rather than "negativity" or "pain" because it's simply a part of daily life. Eating food and drinking fluid creates waste … that's what we have bathrooms for. Living life in a connected manner creates waste energy, and that is what we have Emotional Processing for. If we don't process, waste energy leads to something very different.

This analogy is going to be messy, but I have found it accurate, and I really want it taken seriously.

Imagine that you and your significant other (or roommate, or family that you live with) are living life followed around by a toddler in a diaper. Imagine that you each go to work and come home and go about daily activities with a toddler next to you. Imagine that the normal waste energy of daily life is symbolized as physical waste filling up the diaper of the little guy or gal next to you. How long do we put off changing the diaper? What happens if we rush it? What happens if we for-get? What happens if we get upset by multiple things in a row and the diaper overflows? What happens if we trigger waste energy in our partner and that triggers waste energy in us?

Crap gets everywhere. Not sexy, and likely damaging to the Relationship House if it happens often enough.

But what does this look like?

I come home in a crabby mood and meet my sweet wom-an with a crabby tone while she's happy and sweetly cooking dinner for everyone. Now my toddler has kicked her toddler ... and we both have to process. She didn't deserve that, and I know it, so now my toddler is carrying an even bigger load because of the guilt. This kind of thing can easily become a cycle that will last the entire evening, *just because I didn't stop to change a diaper.*

This is why one of the most basic things to learn as an adult is **Emotional Potty-Training**. This is just a basic descrip-tion of *not letting the crap that happened to us during the day become the crap that gets our entire house messy.*

So, how are we at this? On a scale of one to ten?

Take a moment and think of your life. Think about your youth, early adulthood, and now your 70s (maybe not that far along). Think of how good at cleaning up after yourself you have been, and rate yourself. We're not supposed to be perfect; life is messy, and situations get messier the more we change and grow. For instance, living alone or with my Dad, I was really good at it because nothing was going on. Now if I'm good at it, it's because I'm working my butt off. I'd give myself a healthy 7 right now. We should know where we are, even if it's just for our own personal reality-checking purposes.

The 3D world is non-negotiable and waste energy is non-negotiable in an engaged life. Where that energy ends up depends solely on our personal ability to process emotion. Thus, the relationship's overall success will have a LOT to do with how both parties process emotion. This is just how the world works--or in most cases, doesn't.

There is a lot to take on here, in the world of emotional volatility and activation. But we do have more opportunities to engage and process if we are working TOGETHER than if we are on our own. This is why many of the questions on the speed dating checklist are there, to see if we're going to be alone in this, or if we are going to have a teammate. Having a teammate is helpful, because they can **Hold Space** for us as we Process Emotion.

Having a teammate does not only make Processing Emotion an easier task to complete, it creates a relationship of greater depth and richness.

Holding Space ... and What Is Difficult About It

Holding Space is the act of disengaging from our own emotional reactivity long enough to provide an environment without consequences for another person who is processing "at or near" us. We do this because emotional venting/outbursts/distress are often a ***birthing-process-precursor to heightened awareness and peace*** ... and we believe that possible enlightened eventuality is worth protecting, even if it means we have to do some maneuvering. That is why we do it … we protect the possible growth of the Divine Other. This means we need to do one of two things.

1) We find a *perspective* that is not emotionally reactive to the situation (easier with strangers).

2) We use all the effort we have to *consistently dismiss any internal reactivity* that would interrupt whatever process we are trying to allow.

Generally speaking, it is best to find a perspective to switch into. It's usually possible to create one if one does not come to us naturally. "Usually." Actively dismissing means that we are going to have to go back to the thoughts and reactions we dismissed and process them later. More of a pain, but still very doable, and easier with practice.

This, however, is not what makes Holding Space difficult. The difficulty in Holding Space is not in the "act of Holding Space" … the difficulty in Holding Space is "**Realizing NOW is the time we NEED to Hold Space for someone**." The most powerful and important processes are usually those that catch us completely off guard and overwhelm us. If it overwhelms our partner, it is likely going to overwhelm us, too.

Unfortunately for all of us, we don't get to sit down and discuss what crazy emotional reaction from stored trauma is going to come up and how we're going to deal with it. We get to be going about our day when "BAM!!" … now everything is sideways and scary and painful.

The first thing to overcome when realizing that we need to hold space is the ability to not take the distress of our partner as a personal attack. This is really difficult. We IDENTIFY with our partner's comfort and peace. We do. We also have a tendency to want to stop the pain within them by "solving" it. This is not just men who are on "protection duty," but any person who is going to be unsettled by the emergence of a powerful emotional outpouring.

"Stop crying or I'll give you something to cry about."

"Don't complain; people elsewhere have it way worse than you."

"When I was a kid, we didn't have food; we had to eat garbage." (That's true.)

These are all examples of *parents not wanting to hold space for their kids.* You may be thinking, "Yeah, but some kids are whiny and need to be more appreciative" … true. Really, it's true about most all kids in this country. But that doesn't mean we tell them to *repress their emotion because it's making us uncomfortable.* We listen, quietly, allowing them to have their emotional process; then we get proactive if we want them to become empowered.

For some reason, with adults, we don't think this is the same. It is. Adults, if healthy, will go through the same emotional processes as kids and need the same type of respect. Why do adults and kids go through the same processes? In general, it's because, as adults, the emotional distresses are greater than anything we could have had when we were kids. We get older, the stresses get more distressing. Same process is needed to clear the *new and upgraded stressor.* The average stresses of a child vs. the average stresses of a parent? Not equal. So yes … we still need people to hold space for us and we need to hold space for others. We need to protect growth processes whenever we can.

How do we do it? How do we know when it's the right time to hold space and switch perspectives/dismiss reactivity? We assume it. We observe what energy is flowing through someone having a moment of activation, and we make the best guess. In general, if someone is activated at all it's best to begin Holding Space right away. If we know them and pay attention to how they process, this should not be rocket science.

But ... what if we can't? What if we're activated about something else or having our own issues and can't switch perspectives? Then we can't. It's a missed opportunity to provide safety, create trust, and grow. It's a loss. Bummer.

But ... what if we can't over a long period of time? Then odds are high that the whole "relationship" thing is not going to work out very well for us.

It's a skill. It doesn't happen by magic. It's not something some people are just perfect at and don't have to work at. It's work. And the more we are invested in someone, the harder it is to not be reactive when they are activated. Yes, it's harder. But we should also be more motivated to learn how to do this ... and in the end, that's how we all end up getting skilled at relationship stuff ... by being motivated by deep and rich emotion.

There are a million reasons relationships work and don't work. There are so many things I talk about in this book alone that lead to success and loss. But of all the many things I talk about, few are as cut and dried as Processing Emotion. Being able to do it, and allowing space for others to do it, will always lead to an overall improvement of life. Not being able to do it will always be *one* of the reasons reason things crash and burn.

It's a skill, though. Have no doubt about it. It needs to be focused on and practiced ... and even then, there is no guarantee we're going to be able to manage situations every time.

Chapter 19:

Depth Means Discomfort ...

As I looked at this chapter when it was coming up on my "to-do" list, I realized that it is basically the back half of an earlier chapter ... Chapter 8. "The cave you fear to enter holds the treasure you seek." That chapter was focused on the deep discovery of slowly removing all the shielding briars around a human heart so that depth and intimacy could be achieved. This chapter is about the *maintenance of that intimacy* and what types of challenges it creates over the course of a "really long time."

ALL THE THINGS!

We are going to be affected by the history of our Divine Other and the specific genetics in their body. This is not a choice we make; it is just *the reality of being connected*. Their exes? Their hard childhood? Their broken hearts? Their addictions? Their rejections? Their phobias? Their tendency toward diabetes or heart failure? Their digestive needs? Their scars? Every car accident? Their credit history? Their job? Their family's money issues, physical and psychological? Their family constellation issues? Their ancestral behavioral DNA? Their past lives?

THOSE ARE ALL OURS NOW. All ours.

I have mentioned "wanting everything" enough in this book to make it appealing (I hope), and maybe enough times that you as the reader are motivated to try to get into that mindset of looking forward to that challenge. If you are, then honestly I feel like I've done what I set out to do in writing this.

So ... now let me tell you all the reasons that taking on that attitude is going to be frustratingly difficult over the long haul.

1) **It's always going to be on us** to take the brunt of it. Once we achieve intimacy beyond all others in our partner's life and a connection at the deepest level, it is only we who will be dealing with whatever comes up. There is no therapist, regardless of their title, that can make the mess within our Divine Other "not ours to deal with."

    It may be that this weight is indirect. It may be that traumas and traits from their past generate impulsive behaviors that generate debt or trouble where we live. It may be directed at us and it may not. It may be that each time we say an everyday word that a previous abuser would say to them that we get the wrath of hell sent in our direction for no other reason than we were momentarily careless. Heck, it may not have even been us that said the everyday word. Still, it is ours.

2) **It never ends**. There is no finish line when it comes to traumas and the depths of pain we carry with us, personally, so there is no final relief for it when it comes to our partners. If something from their past comes up ... then we are affected. EVERY TIME. To not be affected means that we are not connected. The only hope is that we have

learned well enough to *anticipate* and *adjust* and *process* very quickly and efficiently. If we are doing our homework and keeping ourselves motivated, this is not *that* difficult. Difficult, yes … but not *that* difficult.

3) **Because it is uncomfortable, uncontrollable, and unceasing, it is very difficult to stay positive about it** … yet, any refusal on our part to manage and work with the deep realities our Divine Other is a ***deep rejection of their being***. Because while it is not THEM … it is a *part of them* that they cannot separate from themselves. Again, regardless of how we think it should be, *this is how life is*.

4) **It goes both ways.** My issues are always going to affect my mate. I have PTSD and social anxiety and am bipolar. There is never going to be a day where that doesn't affect her life in a meaningful way. *I have to be okay with that*. It's not easy. It's much easier to want to sabotage and separate from her so that she doesn't feel my pain and is not burdened by worrying about me. That can't be done without severing ties … so I have to sit and watch her get hurt or worried when I'm in distress, and there's nothing I can do about it most of the time. My only job is to try to manage my own stuff and my guilt over affecting her as much as I can *so that I don't make it worse*. And from my years doing therapy in these areas … ***almost everyone makes it worse***. Until they learn otherwise, of course. Which leads us to …

5) **We cannot indulge frustration.** "The first rule of holes: If you find yourself in one, *stop digging*." Indulging whatever momentary frustration we have will make it worse, and so that's the first rule … don't make it worse. Our natural tendency to indulge our frustration will always be

an option when something comes up. Anger Transference becomes tough to stop when we indulge ourselves in this way. This, in my opinion, is one reason why some couples just scream at each other. They are both using a momentary activation to scream at people in their past by using the person now as an agent for their presence.

So, even if it's the 50th time something has happened, we don't get to be all bothered about it IF we want to continue to have a healthy level of intimacy.

"I want all of it." We must remember we said it as we move forward into the intimidating depths of connection with our Divine Other. In my experience, the issues we have "in general" get better over time and our reactivity gets "less violent" overall. IN GENERAL and OVERALL are the main words there. Everyone is different. But that's the good news (in case you needed some).

This is a good thing, *even though it's wearing a barbed wire shirt and asking for a hug*. Life, in general, asks us to move forward into some pretty frightening and painful realities. As we expand and grow, that doesn't change. When I was a child, my brother was battling cancer for many years (still battling, thirty years later). That was quite a challenge at every stage of my youthful development. But I was lucky in that I learned an amazing lesson very early. Life was going to challenge me. It was simply part of life. It was going to be messy and frightening, and I was going to have to respond to violent changes often. I learned to embrace it. I did it for myself and my family. It was good for my mental health and made the challenges my family were facing a little bit easier for them. A little ... it was still cancer.

In that same way, we can embrace the reality that exists within our Divine Other. My brother had cancer; there was no way around that. I could work with it the best I could…or not. Our Divine Others have histories. We can work with that the best we can… or not. I have PTSD and social anxiety among a myriad of other issues. My mate can embrace that…or not. *It's easier for both of us when she does*.

Embracing the possibility of pain and keeping ourselves from clenching up when we have to deal with it coming to the surface can make a world of difference in our relationships with everyone. We don't have to like it, **but we can honor it as part of the process of being deeply and intimately involved with another person**. There is nothing that says "I love you" as much as the willingness to embrace all the chaos that resides within someone. *The willingness to engage … it goes a long way*.

Chapter 20:

If You Don't Think They'd Be Kind Through a Divorce, Don't Marry Them

There are going to be very few places in this book where I flat-out give advice, but this is one area I have a particular attachment to. I am a fan of divorce. This does not mean I like when marriages fail. I am simply a fan of change and refinement. I like that people can grow apart, and I like that people can recognize it and take appropriate action. I like it.

What I don't like? I don't like unnecessary suffering. I really, really, REALLY don't like it. Divorces are painful enough without them being the breeding grounds for interpersonal brutality and willful destruction. When they get malicious, they become *the obscenity of social reality* in what is otherwise a "sorta" civilized world.

70%

That's the number. 70 out of 100. That's how many couples that tie the knot will fork over thousands to a lawyer someday to legally split. I think if we can get socially active in promoting Processing Emotion, we can get that number down quite a bit. That, however, is not my mission in this chapter. My mission in this chapter is to get everyone, every single person, to ask themselves some questions about someone they are thinking of marrying.

I want us to do this, not only because it will give us a perspective on a possible future we may have to live through, but because *the investigative effort* to follow through with the questions *will tell us a TON* about the person we are thinking about tying our futures to. Some of us can imagine divorce easily. For others, it is more difficult to do so. If it is difficult, here are some questions to ponder that may help.

1) How have our partner's relationships generally ended, and how do they speak of their exes?

2) When our partner has nothing to lose in a situation where they are frustrated but have to take part anyway, are they honorable in their behavior, or spiteful and vengeful?

3) On a scale of one to ten, how devoted to our health and future is our partner?

4) Does our partner value our contribution to the world, or just our contribution to them? Both? Which do they value more?

5) When things aren't going well, how often do they lash out at others? (Because once divorced, we are the primary acceptable target and likely recipient.)

The statement "I knew they were capable of it, I just didn't know they were capable of doing it to me" does not excuse us anymore. Our partners may not be capable of doing it to us when things are going well, but when they are desperate and angry, we can be SURE that they are capable of doing it to us.

These are questions we should be asking ourselves anyway, as they help define the character of a human being, but they definitely paint a picture of how things will go if a split becomes inevitable. If children are involved, the stakes get raised by 10,000%. When kids are involved, we are going to be stuck dealing with custody until they turn eighteen. That's no joke. That is being stuck with someone and having to trust their parenting for a long time. That can be "easy co-parenting" or "spending a decade and 50 grand in court trying to justify your existence to strangers." The horror stories are real. So are the success stories. If we ask these questions, we are going a long way to making sure which one we are going to be in.

Don't be afraid to think about eventualities. I could say "Don't be afraid of death, because you will die no matter what." But I am saying "Don't be afraid to think of how things could go wrong, *because they may go wrong simply because you never asked yourself the question.*"

Chapter 21:

Resentment, the Mess, and the Point of No Return

This is a weird chapter. It's a chapter about recognizing when we've blown it. I personally believe "relationship closures" are all learning experiences and that they serve a deeper purpose to draw us ever closer to the person we are going to be with in the future and *the person we are going to be with them*.

Not everyone has the reaction that I have. In fact, most people, would rather pretend like everything is fine rather than realize the Relationship House is condemned. This … costs … people … years. Lord.

The truth of the matter is that there is an invisible line … a point of no return. This is when the amount of resentment being held within the people in the relationship (one or both) is greater than those carrying it can hope to process … EVER. This is when things start to go bad and relationships start *bringing out the worst* in people. We've all seen it. We've all likely been in it. It's awful, and it's TOTALLY UNNECESSARY.

There is a way to stop this from happening. Unfortunately, it's not something we are taught to do. It's twice as difficult to try to do something we aren't taught to do, *when that thing is hard on our ego*. But **throwing in the towel when the dance has devolved into a brawl** is exactly what we need to get better at doing. For everyone's sake.

From Dance Floor to Boxing Ring ... Resentment at Its Finest

None of us are born dancers, and not all of us are meant to dance together. This is the truth, and it's okay. It's OKAY. I believe much of the way relationships are spoken about leads us to extend them into dangerous territories ... because it ties them to an idea of success and failure based on whether it lasts forever, rather than how much joy and growth was achieved.

This may seem obvious and maybe trivial. What I see, though, is people extending relationships past the point of no return because they're afraid of a perceived failure, and in doing so the two people involved actually DESTROY EACH OTHER. This is insane.

"Instead of admitting failure ... I'd rather destroy us both." That's what we're saying when we stay in relationships past the point of no return. It's obscene, and it can stop.

The first thing we need to do is make an internal agreement with ourselves to recognize and honor it. Then, once we get this focus into the arena of relationships, we may be able to see the truth. The END of a relationship and the SUCCESS of a relationship are in NO WAY CONNECTED.

I've had successful relationships last less than an hour ... the growth involved was expansive and it imprinted on my being. I've seen marriages dissolve into disrepair that were NONETHELESS great successes.

What makes something NOT a success? Deep resentment and anger that we carry with us going forward, distressing our hearts and closing our energies off to opportunities because we are carrying garbage. And when we overcome those, they end up being successes too.

So how do we get to this atrocious state? Think of a dance floor.

When we enter into a union with another person, there is a lot of excitement and learning. There is a lot of patience, as well as the minimizing of differences and the value of any new form of contact. This is beautiful. In order to keep the dance going as best we can, it is important to make the most of changes and maximize the positive aspects of the encounter.

But ... that takes skill and courage and experience and a natural chemistry between the dancers. It doesn't happen all that often.

What happens often?

Frustration.   Miscommunication.   Accidental   injury. Clumsiness.

That happens, and until we are professionals at processing these minor momentary pains, they become *weaponized* within us.

So, after each dance, each partner regroups. After many dances and many misfires on the dance floor, the partners come out not with the intent to have a great dance, but to dance and injure the other. Imagine it ... really take a moment. Imagine two people coming together for a dance, and while they are dancing they are trying to nonchalantly step on each other's toes or kick each other's shins. For the record, most relationships I see are in this stage ... *when they are going well*. Honestly, it's not bad in comparison to what comes next.

After causing some injury and continuing to dance, the intents change. The primary goal becomes inflicting injury … and the dance becomes secondary. This is the moment when resentment's presence has been validated and has begun to dominate our mindset. This is the spot where we need to see the red flags raising so that we can try to stop it. It's possible but unlikely to come back from this point. It's likely best to walk away. But we generally don't, and it generally gets much worse.

I'll say this again … the moment that we enter into a shared situation with the subtle intent to hurt the one we're in union with, that's when the damn relationship is basically over. Got it? If we can't see that, then we're the worst kind of careless. If we refuse to see it, then we are earning all the garbage we go through and shouldn't be legally allowed to complain about any of it without risking jail time.

It's obvious that I'm a tad emotional about it.

The next stage is outright battle. There is no dancing. Both parties come out of regrouping in a boxer's stance. Attack and defend, blow by blow, the relationship devolves into a blood-bath with both parties caring little for their own health and mostly about the damage they can inflict to resurrect a sense of power and righteousness. There is no excuse for this as a human being. But … it's so common that society still accepts it rather than alarm bells going off.

This ends up with both bloodied and immobilized. Damaged. This is not okay. It is NOT the eventuation of loving attraction we want to be the *primary story in our culture*. We can change this. Like, literally, you reading this, can change this.

We just have to commit to recognizing it, and loving ourselves and our divine other enough to walk away when it has.

Every relationship has its mess. The mess of a relationship is the natural byproduct of the changes of both people involved in the relationship. If there's no mess, there likely isn't any changing going on. If there's no changing going on, there likely isn't much of a relationship.

We all have things we are working toward as human beings. We all have new wants and desires and focuses coming up all of the time, and there is always going to be conflict ... this is normal. HOW THAT CONFLICT GETS PLAYED OUT IN THE RELATIONSHIP HOUSE is of huge importance.

These messes can be handled and resolved ... digested by the relationship as a foundation for further strength in the future ... or they can become rocks in our shoes that eat away at us. The tough thing is, we may not be able to control whether we are taking on resentment and frustration. We may be totally fine with an aging or ill partner when we're young, and that may totally change as we get older. We do not get to decide for our future selves how we are going to feel throughout the many changes we are going to go through. This can be a real bummer when people begin to change and their paths begin to separate.

The reason we want recognition is because there is a point of no return. I alluded to it in the dance floor to boxing ring analogy, but it deserves a little more attention, because it is precisely these moments we want to try to prevent from happening. If we can't prevent them from happening, we want to at least be able to know that they happened so we can take appropriate action.

The Point of No Return

Have you ever been in a fight or argument in a relationship, and one of you says something, and a huge bell goes off in your head screaming "Yep, that's all she wrote!"

I have. My bet is that you have, too. We don't want to admit it, but we know it happened. We're not going to be able to put what was said behind us. This means every hug and every sexual encounter is going to have whatever was said stuck in between the two of us. That's not fun.

Some relationships we are too deeply tied up in to be able to get out quickly, and we have to ride them to some violent finish line. Logically, I don't get that, but my heart tells me it's a needed lesson when it does happen. It's good to know. I've had it happen six months into a sixteen-month relationship. The knowledge helped me prepare for what would end up happening (I lost everything, including my health and almost my life) so that I could at least salvage something of my world when things eventually exploded.

The "point of no return" often speaks to us. As I got older I began to really respect that voice as the powerful ally that it was. I also started going back through my relationships trying to figure out the other times it had spoken to me, so that I could remember its voice, and possibly describe it to others.

In truth, this voice is speaking through a well of resentment that is too deep for us to ever get out of. It is trying to tell us that our hearts and minds are becoming twisted and perverted forms of themselves because of the resentment being held.

How do we know? We know when we get happy when the one we love fails, or is in pain. This is often a very subtle thing at first. So subtle it can be going on quietly for months before it starts to get loud, in the same way an angry drunk at a bar will be muttering to himself for an hour before he cold cocks someone he takes a disliking to. And while there may be something that can be done about it in the early stages if we catch it, there is absolutely nothing we can do after we have validated our cruelty consciously.

Why do I say that? If we really love them, *we can't handle the guilt.* Then, we will resent them not for whatever we resented them for that caused the initial issue, *but for the guilt we feel now* that we are constantly reminded of our own violence. That's besides the fact that they may enact vengeance upon us, which creates the boxing ring analogy we were dealing with earlier.

The point of no return can be anywhere and happen at any time. It can also be very far past where we expect it to be or much earlier than we expect it to be. We can't know when we first start out. We have to learn. Much more than learning, though? We have to extend where that spot is by processing our garbage and pushing our limits.

Why must we do this? Because the odds of reaching the point of no return are ungodly high. I'd wager about 95% of serious relationships from where I am sitting now end up there. It may seem high, but we are a species *that has not yet placed a premium value on quality of life.* As a result, our quality of life kinda sucks. The funny thing about how high that number is … is that a relationship can end in a breakup and not hit the point of no return if both parties are conscious and caring of each other. So the percentage doesn't need to be ANYWHERE NEAR THAT HIGH. I could be wrong. It may not be that high … but if I had to lay down a number to win a jar full of candy corn, 95% is what I'd pick.

It's really hard to keep it from happening ... resentment. And it's harder to stop it from snowballing once it starts. The hardest thing, though, is living with having been in a "brutalizing" relationship ... a relationship that devolved into the destruction of both parties.

This is serious. We are ruining human beings that we love (and ourselves) simply by not being careful in this, the most tender of arenas. And it's not going to stop by itself. Attraction will continue to bring us together and the inability to manage ourselves in union will tear us to shreds ... over and over. So, we really need to learn to manage these unions. The moments where we can make a decision and prevent damage? The moments we can take a breath and a step back? We need to get to know these moments and get comfortable ***acting in harmony with our integrity when they happen***.

Chapter 22:

The Desperate Need for Stupid Trust

Trust is stupid. It's also necessary.

I know of very few other aspects of connecting with others that captures the same aspects of frustrating insanity that this simple truth does.

If we trust someone, the pain and humiliation of our trust not being fulfilled is truly devastating. If we, on the other hand, cannot move ourselves to employ trust, then the rewarding aspects of connection are basically nullified. Basically, it's like winning a delicious dinner by burning our taste buds off.

This is the entire basis of creating union, though. We have to try to trust. If we succeed, it's going to hurt. It's going to hurt even if our trust-hopes are fulfilled. If they are not fulfilled, then it is *really going to hurt*.

So how are we going to motivate ourselves to walk down an avenue that guarantees pain? Everyone has their own way, I'd guess. For me? I wanted to feel alive more than I wanted to protect myself. And goodness gracious, I paid the price. Many times.

But Did You Die?

I didn't. I have been burned badly. I have been burned badly enough to figure that I was done trying. I have even had relationships where trust was not really an issue by design (long distance, didn't have to trust my ability to live with them).

But these periods always ended. That darn spark was still lively and pulling me forward.

Each time I regained my strength to reach out and connect, I knew that the odds were low of it working out and that I had to give it everything I had.

How did I convince myself to do it after all those failures? I realized that I didn't die. That's pretty much it. I was humiliated, betrayed, hurt, abandoned, rejected, and even assaulted. But ... no death. So here I still was.

"What am I going to do now?" I'd ask myself each time, and each time the answer was always "Keep trying as hard as I can." Truthfully ... that's dumb.

"How many times does a hot stove have to burn me before I start protecting myself?" I would ask myself in response to my continued stubbornness. "There is no limit to how many times I am willing to be burned for this" was my response. Still kinda dumb.

Whoever you are, reading this, enjoying these final chapters with me wherever you are lucky enough to have some spare reading time, you are alive. Whatever happened to you, regardless of how badly it damaged you and broke your trust and expectations ... it didn't kill you.

There is no mincing words about what I am suggesting. I am asking you to walk toward pain open-armed. I am asking you to walk into the meat grinder. I am asking you, also, to look stupid while you're doing it. Trusting anyone in this chaotic world is naïve ... so when you look at yourself doing it? You're going to look stupid. I'm asking you to do that, and accept that, too.

One of the reasons I am making this my point (the looking stupid part), is that there are situations we're going to be in that are going to demand we go all the way even when we know logically it's not going to work. We have to do this in order to honor and satisfy our hearts. We have to. Ignoring logic and looking stupid ... we have to.

Going All the Way, Lesson-Learning for Love ...

I wrote this about three years ago ...

The feminine is in a cycle where she goes toward someone but doesn't fully let go (into the relationship) because the person isn't good for her.

In this case, the heart says: "I want that one." The mind goes *halfway* and realizes there's an issue ... then *the mind tries to pull out and protect the heart*. As a result, the heart doesn't learn the lesson.

Imagine this: It's like your heart picked out candy, and as it was about to eat it your mind realized you were allergic to an ingredient and then stopped your heart from eating.

Your mind knows it would have sent you to the hospital,

BUT YOUR HEART DOESN'T. *Your heart only knows YOU stopped it from having the candy.*

You have to let your heart have the candy and get sick. It has to get DEMOLISHED to learn. Fully. Completely. Demolished. Then you can be reborn into a new type of desire. *Until then your heart will just want the candy your brain hasn't let you have.* This really damages any heart-brain trust in your body and becomes a serious upset to the system as a whole.

The assumption that we are in charge of our desire is incorrect and the idea that we can boss our heart around is false and rude. Trying to do so shows our great lack of respect for and humility for the human heart and its characteristics.

We have to trust. It's dumb most of the time and won't work out a really high percentage of the time … we have to do it anyway. I am reiterating this because it is really hard to not sabotage relationships and pull our hearts out early. It is really hard to be present in a state of doubt and risk, where we are exposed, and continue to walk open and naked toward what could end up being a bath of thorns.

Ever heard these?

"I have a hard time trusting people." Of course, everyone does.

"I'm afraid of getting hurt." Of course, everyone is.

"I am not good at opening up." I know, not really newsworthy.

"I was hurt." Yep, I know.

What we have to do is put an addendum on the end of the sentence that is implied. The addendum is: "… so I stopped risking because I'm a coward, even though I really want to connect."

So, I'm suggesting, maybe … that we get sick of our own

scaredy-cat bullshit a little earlier in life. I'm suggesting we live, and do so fully, without the guarantee of comfort or success.

I can tell you from experience that it's emboldening and satisfying. I can also tell you from experience that it hurts. And while I can't be sure that I will have no regrets on my deathbed, I can tell you that I certainly don't have any now.

Chapter 23:

INTERDEPENDENCE

"If you wish to travel fast, travel alone. If you wish to travel far, travel together." – African Proverb

I quoted this in my last book, and I am doing so again in this one to reiterate the importance of it from another angle. There are *so many things we want to do* in this life and there are *so many obstacles* to overcome internally and externally. Such is the nature of a chaotic, co-created, incarnated life.

In *Coffee for Consciousness 101*, when I mentioned this, I was talking about forming a relationship with our emotional matrix so that feelings could inspire us and love could be integrated for resonance. The downside was that we would have to face and form a relationship with fear, sadness, and anger as well. This is a tough thing that, once undertaken, is the most internally rewarding thing we can ever do in this life.

In this book, I am talking about forming a relationship with another human being. In this life, there is no more *externally* rewarding thing we can do. I say that without hesitation.

No matter what area of life we are looking at … career, life purpose, sexuality, artistry, expression, knowledge, self-awareness, joy, depth and variance of experience … they are all more easily accomplished when we are not working alone. When we are supported. When our growth is the integral part of another person's caring focus and energy.

What Is Interdependence?

Interdependence is NOT codependence. I will write more on that in another section, but let's just get that taken care of right off the bat.

Interdependence, in a relationship, is the union of two whole individuated beings. In today's world, this is beyond rare. We may see it in healthy work environments between coworkers "to attain a specific work goal." Even that is rare. Have you seen it anywhere?

Have you been in a work or school environment where the project's welfare was the driving motivational force behind all behavior? Have you experienced when two or more people can work together in honor of a desired outcome or creation?

My first experience of it was in a band, writing songs. I also enjoyed it at a couple really awesome jobs (waiting tables can bring out the best in people). In those situations, the goal was "writing songs and doing an album" and "getting through the night with as few mistakes as possible so we could split a higher amount of tips between everyone." Those are simple goals.

When we look at Interdependence in a relationship setting … the goal is personal expansion and self-actualization. Holy shit, is THAT different. It's abstract. There are no real rules, and if there are, they are likely changing and evolving over time as the people involved change. There are very few models for it in our society, and even if there were models aplenty, it wouldn't help, because everyone is different and their reality is unlikely to fully apply to ours.

Interdependence is trusting our relationship with ourselves and another person so much that we are willing to go forward *within* the relationship without any external validation or justification for how we behave and relate to each other from *outside* the relationship. That's freaking scary. ***An autonomous unit working together to actualize and expand the individuals within it***. Sounds kinda sexy, doesn't it? Not needing anything but each other? That's Interdependence.

There is too much in any one person for them to be able to engage all of it on their own. Heck, some things within us we can't even know about until we are in situations with other people and they draw it out of us. If we want to fully grow and engage self-awareness, depending on other human beings is necessary (hopefully people on the same journey).

We want this to be healthy Interdependence, though. We do not want *the guise of interdependence* to actually be *the stasis of codependence* and the forming of the betrayal bond that exists between so many who have opted into situations that trap them. Situations that trap them within their own prisons and keep them *excused from participating* in the destructive and creative chaos of growth as well as excusing them from their own accountability for freeing themselves and becoming sovereign.

That last paragraph was kind of as mouthful, but you get the point, right? Some people get enmeshed so they can hide from themselves and escape accountability for their lack of growth. That's really not what we're after.

Codependence vs. Interdependence

Codependence: I am incomplete and I need you to not change, because I don't want to change … even if it is a betrayal of my basic drive as a conscious being.

Interdependence: I am complete and my need is for you to willingly and consciously support my growth because I am going to keep changing and I want to do so healthily.

Codependence: There are no real consequences for behavior because we need each other more than we honor our integrity, so transgressions may lead to drama, but not to change. That means there's no real risk … and our egoic mind can bask in safety.

Interdependence: Every move and every action has a consequence that affects both parties. These consequences will definitely lead to a change in behavior, whether the consequences are good or bad, as each reaction creates a new dynamic within the couple.

Codependence: The relationship forms our identity, and I am a servant to the needs of stasis within it.

Interdependence: We form our individual identities, and we both work to preserve the integrity of those identities as they evolve over time.

Codependence: One addict, one enabler.

Interdependence: Two addicts getting sober together.

Codependence: Generally complains to outsiders about how they're trapped and unsatisfied to reinforce the power of the enmeshment.

Interdependence: Doesn't need outsiders at all. They may brag on being happy or share some of the goals they have, but there's no reason to seek guidance elsewhere. The other person is our best ally for that.

Codependence: Two unhealthy people latching on to each other's wounds to keep each other sickly and weak.

Interdependence: Two healthy people cleaning each other's wounds and trying to get healthy.

Codependence: I want my mate to be weak so they will never leave me ... and I'm willing to cripple them to achieve this.

Interdependence: I want my mate strong so we can do things together, even if they leave me as a result.

Codependence: My mate will believe my bullshit, because calling me on it would threaten their bullshit when they need to use it.

Interdependence: My mate will call me on my bullshit and expects me to call them on theirs.

Why would we call each other out? Why do we push each other?

Because we honor the soul residing in the other person. We honor it above our comfort and above our safety. The ideal of who we are becoming as individuated souls is simply more important than our momentary comfort.

What if we all honored it? What if we all saw ourselves working together on a group project and the group project was each other's soul expansion? We totally can, you know. It's not impossible at all.

Perspective Shifting into Interdependence ... the Class Assignment

Our integrity is connected to more than our momentary perspectives. In order to stay aligned with it through the chaos, we are going to have to learn how to step out of a MOMENT ... into Observer Consciousness ... and then focus on where we are on the great stage of our intent.

How do we do this?

I have been struggling with analogies for this. It took me a half hour of staring blankly at the ceiling, but I figured out why. THIS SHOULDN'T TAKE AN ANALOGY. "Doing what's best for the person we love" isn't some weird math problem. It's not the SATs. We shouldn't need a prize to inspire added motivation for this. This should be what we naturally want to do.

So what do we do when the growth or change gets uncomfortable and we are trapped in an emotional reality that is preventing us from honoring our Divine Other? We Perspective Shift. Because it's the right thing to do. It's right every time.

This is how we do it.

1) Recognize that we are uncomfortable and at risk for betraying our integrity as it regards the person we are trying to honor.

2) Stop ourselves from acting out.

3) Conjure the part of ourselves that is willing to honor our Divine Other regardless of our own comfort. It's there. This isn't something we have to build; it's just something we have to remember. It's the "deeply in love" and "so fresh it still has the new car smell" perspective.

4) Listen to the voice of that perspective and FEEL the love that is generating its identity. FEEL THE LOVE THAT IS GENERATING ITS IDENTITY. That loving self exists outside our bullshit. Step INTO that perspective FULLY.

5) Now it's time to *honor* and *validate* that part of our being by *acting in harmony* with its goals. Our egoic mind will whine … we can shut that garbage down immediately.

If it was a high school class project, we'd set aside our momentary issues with whoever we were in class with so that we could get a good grade. This is the person we love, not a stranger in 11th grade Chem. And this is the health and growth of our SOUL, not a freaking grade.

That is why comparing this to any other analogy is ridiculous. It's the most important thing in the world, comparing it to LITERALLY ANYTHING ELSE is disrespectful to the point of being obscene.

Angry? Sad? Freaked out? Exhausted? Overworked? Underappreciated? Yeah?

Those momentary states pale in comparison to *the commitment to honor another human being's soul*. Period. This is the "deeply loving" part of ourselves we are nurturing into a more full presence each time we use it.

When we have two people doing this in a relationship … we have magic. We have meaning. We have purpose. And we have satisfaction. Honestly … I don't know that there's more to life than knowing that feeling from having lived it. There may be, but I haven't found it.

Interdependence is a step. It is an evolutionary step for our species that gains momentum and traction each time we can engage it and follow through with it. Is it easy? No. Are the actions to take always obvious and easy to discern? No … in fact sometimes there are no answers at all. None of that matters. The success or failure in this realm does not matter. Only our commitment to it does.

It's again time for you to stop and ask yourself, "Who do I want to be?"

Chapter 24:

APPLY ME.

When I say "APPLY ME" I don't just mean "Think about the tools in this book and try to use them." I mean something more along the lines of "Read the most important parts of this book out loud to the person you're interested in and see how they respond." I mean "Commit to certain perspectives and principles you've seen in this book and refer back to them throughout your relationship." I mean "Use this book as a guide to REFINING your relationships AS THEY ARE HAPPENING."

Apply it. Put the book into your relationship. Hold YOURSELF accountable for living up to it and ask your Divine Other to do the same.

Love FEELS magical ... but learning how to love IS NOT MAGIC. It is knowledge, focus, and effort, all working in a Divine Union within us and our fueled by our CONTINUED commitment to ***honoring the love we feel***.

It Doesn't Matter Who You Are ...

The best and scariest things about love all come in the same explosive package. Regardless of who we love or how we are connected, we can learn to honor that love more fully. Everyone in the world that is drawing breath right now can learn how to love better. This is the opportunity we ALL share. We all share this because honoring love involves opening the heart and risking pain ... *for everyone.*

It doesn't matter if we are in prison in an isolation unit. It doesn't matter if we are stranded on a desert island. It doesn't matter if we are in the perfect relationship and are totally happy and satisfied. We can ALL get better at *being in relation to those we love.* We can ALL get better at integrating the relationships we have with ourselves. Our inner child, our emotions, our desires ... all.

I don't remember when it dawned on me. It may have been when I was in a long-distance relationship in my twenties or just after a heartbreaking ending to a relationship in my later twenties. I realized that I could *just be a good boyfriend.* I could be a good partner. I realized that I didn't need to do anything superlative or have a specifically spectacular identity. I could just be "good" ... and that was enough. It turns out that it's actually a *lot,* rather than just "enough."

So, I started trying. I literally, for the first real time in my life, started trying to be good. I realized it wasn't that complicated. *It was HARD sometimes.* But it wasn't *complicated.* And because it wasn't complicated, I found that I ended up having more energy and enjoying things more. Then I got confident and ended up with *even more energy.*

The truth is that everyone can be good. It's definitely harder for some people. Some people have a TON to work through. Some people have serious disadvantages. But we can all do it. We can all apply our care for the world to our behaviors in such a way that we honor ourselves and the world in the process of moving through it. And that's the idea. Small applications over time become healthy habits. These habits are expressed outward to others through our commitment to them and are attractive because of the satisfaction we get in being their author. We get to wear that ... the satisfaction. For me, that has been more comfortable than anything else I've worn ... much more comfortable than the crazy outfits my egoic mind had me trying on for a decade.

If you're reading this (especially if you have gotten this far), you have already changed. Your perspectives and your opportunities have changed. They have expanded into different possibilities if there is new information, or expanded into connection if you already understood everything you've read. Those are tools of wisdom (regardless of whether you agreed with me or disagreed) ... USE THEM.

Use them when they are at odds with common practice, when they are at odds with old habits, when they are at odds with logic. USE THEM. Everyone can ... everyone has the opportunity to try. It doesn't matter who you are. If you have read this book, you can use it. Bring the unique essence to life through action.

Application is what turns knowledge into wisdom (or proves that knowledge is wisdom, depending on your viewpoint). It is what turns advice into help. It is what turns ideas into habits.

If you didn't like this book? USE THAT.

Let's say that there was too much asked or too many supposed rules. Let's say it was too complex or that you didn't
agree in a major way with parts of this book. AWESOME. USE
THAT, TOO. Know that if you do not like this book for relationships, odds are you need to find someone else who also
didn't like it, and you'll have met a kindred spirit.

If you end up being with someone who *does* like this
book, you may want to look out for the issues I bring up as a
couple and maybe you can find a way to work through them.
That's great, too.

You may not want to do any of this stuff. Maybe someone gave you this book to get you to see what points they
were making, and now you're upset and feel threatened by
the whole thing. GREAT. Now you know **not to move forward
with that relationship**. Truly … if that's what happened, the
two of you want different things. And that's okay.

This book IS FOR PEOPLE WHO WANT TO HAVE THIS
TYPE OF RELATIONSHIP. It's not mandatory for life, just for being happily cohesive in a relationship *with one of the people who
like this book*. It doesn't make you a bad person or weak if you
don't want this. But … you can't not want to do the work AND
HAVE THE KIND OF RELATIONSHIP THAT IS DESCRIBED IN
THIS BOOK. Because the work is integral to the relationship in
the same way that water is a prerequisite for surfing.

So if you didn't like this, use that. Let it be a tool.

If you find that you want to be with someone that likes this
book, and your desire to be with them is more powerful than
your resistance to what is written here? You are my freaking
hero. If you do not like this book, but are willing to work with

the principles because of the depth of feeling you have for a man or woman … you are my hero. And thank you.

If you find that you don't like this book or want these things yet … that's TOTALLY fine. You may never want them. You may decide in two weeks that you want them. You may want to try some and not others … GO FOR IT. The goal of this book is happy connection and open-hearted expression. So any little bit you can do to get started with some of it in your life? PLEASE DO.

It's going to be the case that this book is going to find many of you in unhappy places. It's going to find many in unsatisfying relationships and marriages. That's just a reality. We can use that, too.

Serving Goodness of Fit

I'd be lying if I said I had no idea that this book would cause some relationships to end. I have been doing therapy for long enough to know that the things I talk about lead to life changes. I have witnessed many. I consider such endings a rebirth and reconfiguration of society into a healthier version of itself. A version where happiness and growth and desire are honored over obligation and servitude and expectation. A society where quality of life is valued … *rather than just the presented image of life being valuable.*

These splits will work out for both parties, though it may not seem so at first. It will force the non-dynamic to grow or choose a partner more in tune with their desire for stasis. It will give opportunities of deep growth and loving connection to those who desire a dynamic life by forcing a life change and reimagination of their adult lives.

This is a value I have. Goodness of fit.

If someone doesn't want to change and is with someone who does ... they will never be satisfied or happy, because the other person *will always be changing* ... IT IS WHO THEY ARE. A split saves them that UNENDING DISCOMFORT. And for those that need to be dynamic and ever changing ... it saves their lives to be able to leave and seek what they truly desire. Stasis is not safety for them, it is death.

This difference is okay. It is not a judgment, it is simply allowing reality to be what it is. Everyone is different, and knowing and HONORING these differences is the first step to CELEBRATING the differences. It took me many years to understand those who were different from me, and more years on top to understand that whatever judgments I had about them were inaccurate and disrespectful. They are just different than I am. I don't have to try to change their minds or tell them they are "not good enough" ... I can just not hang out with them. That way, I can enjoy them from afar without our conflicting desires coming into conflict. That's a GOOD thing.

Know this is okay. Change is okay. Finding what we fit with best is okay. Its being painful is okay. Its being difficult is okay. Apply the book. If there are major differences in desire between you and the person you're with ... HONOR THAT by addressing it. That is what love does ... it honors the heart's feelings ... even if it means momentary pain. That is **how love behaves**.

I remember the first time I thought of writing this book. I have had it in my mind since before *Coffee for Consciousness* fully formed, but I had no real idea of when it would be time to write it. I needed something. I needed you.

I am not writing this book just to help people. I am not writing this book just to solve a problem or heal a wound. I am not writing this book just to spread ideas I am deeply connected to, or to promote an agenda to open and unleash the human heart. I am writing this book to you, because I need you to be happier and more fully present. I need it for my kids, for the world, and for my energy … all of which are based in hope. You are that hope.

Your present relationship, your future relationships, what you model for your children … it will literally change the world. I am not being hyperbolic in the slightest. The depth of the connection that can be achieved now with the world the way it is, the empathy that flows from an open, beating heart…this is the only real set of values we need to identify with to move into a golden age.

I waited to write this book because I needed you. You're here now.

What are you going to do?

CPSIA information can be obtained
at www.ICGtesting.com
Printed in the USA
BVHW02s1041111217
502488BV00004B/360/P